R24-133

# THE PRODUCTION

# OF

# CULTURE

Edited by

# Richard A. Peterson

Ⓢ SAGE PUBLICATIONS    *Beverly Hills / London*    1976

The material in this publication originally appeared as a special issue of AMERICAN BEHAVIORAL SCIENTIST (Volume 19, Number 6, July/August 1976). The Publisher would like to acknowledge the assistance of the special issue editor, Richard A. Peterson, in making this edition possible.

*For information address:*

SAGE PUBLICATIONS, INC.
275 South Beverly Drive
Beverly Hills, California 90212

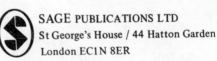

SAGE PUBLICATIONS LTD
St George's House / 44 Hatton Garden
London EC1N 8ER

Printed in the United States of America
International Standard Book Number 0-8039-0734-6
Library of Congress Catalog Card Number 76-41102

**FIRST PRINTING**

Communic.

# CONTENTS

# THE PRODUCTION
# OF
# CULTURE

*Peterson proposes revitalizing the sociology of culture by asking how culture is deliberately produced. Once several inhibitions to comparative analysis are overcome, numerous unexplored communalities in the production of art, science, and religion are revealed. These suggest a genetic theory of the role of culture for society.*

# The Production of Culture

A Prolegomenon

RICHARD A. PETERSON
*Vanderbilt University*

**For a full generation now**, most new developments in sociology have been at the periphery. Substantively defined sociologies of — have proliferated, and a rich load of empirical findings has accumulated. These have been set out in numberless monographs and in a baffling diversity of specialized journals. At the same time, general sociology, grounded as it has been on *a priori* functionalist or Marxist grand theory, has languished. It may now be time to turn more systematically to reworking the central turf of the discipline by building general sociology inductively on a solid empirical base. This can be done by seeking out the conceptual and substantive communalities shared by the diverse substantive specialities. It is in this spirit that we focus on the grand old term "culture."

Reading theoretical essays and introductory texts leads one to suppose that sociologists take culture to be a central concern and view it as closely linked with social structure. In the corpus

**Author's Note:** *Please see note 1 for the history of this research and acknowledgements.*

of sociological research, however, "culture" is focal only in scattered works of individual scholarship. Yet this apparent disinclination to study culture may prove illusory. Although the term is seldom used, a goodly number of us laboring in the sociologies of art, science, religion, knowledge, law, media, education, sports, and popular music *are* researching culture, and doing so in a common way by focusing on how culture is *produced.*

While a reorientation of the sociology of culture around the problem of production may seem an obvious and straightforward proposal, it has not emerged heretofore for several reasons: first, because of the ways in which the society-culture relationship has been conceptualized and, second, because of several characteristic habits of thought which have led workers to compartmentalize and fragment rather than integrate theoretical development and research.[2] These alternative conceptions and blinding habits of thought are discussed in the prolegomenon which follows in order to more clearly define the production-of-culture perspective and to facilitate the search for communalities in the cultural domain.

## THE SOCIETY-CULTURE RELATIONSHIP

Over a century ago, Edward Tylor (1871: 1) defined culture as "that complex whole which includes knowledge, belief, arts, morals, law, custom, and any other capabilities and habits acquired by man as a member of society." While refinements have been made, most authors have accepted this definition (Schneider and Bonjean, 1973) and have focused their attention on the ways in which culture is related to social structure. The empirical locus for addressing this question ranges from face-to-face laboratory groups to entire societies and epochs, but three analytically distinct perspectives can be identified.[3] The first asserts that culture and society are autonomous systems which evolve independently according to quite different rules. At its grandest level, this *autonomous culture cycle* theory can be seen in the work of Sorokin (1937). The perspective has also been taken by persons studying fashion (Kroeber, 1957; Sapir, 1937), styles in art (Bensman and Gerver, 1958), collective behavior (Blumer, 1939), and fads (Meyerson and Katz, 1957).

The second theory is that *social structure creates culture.* This "materialist" view is congenial with the presumption of most sociologists that economic and political factors are the most potent elements defining the structure of society. Within this view, culture is seen as a more or less accurate mirror of social structure so that the content analysis of cultural products provides a convenient unobtrusive measure of social structure (Harap, 1949; Rosenberg and White, 1957; Lowenthal, 1961, 1964; Kavolis, 1968, 1972; Wolfe, 1969; and Denisoff and Peterson, 1972).

The third major perspective is that *culture creates social structure.* This "idealist" position starts from the premise that "in the beginning there was the Word." This position is taken by several otherwise quite different intellectual traditions. They include symbolic interactionists (Duncan, 1968; Klapp, 1969), the humanistically oriented massification theorists (cf. Ortega y Gasset, 1950, MacDonald, 1965; Adorno, 1968), and social linguists and semioticists (cf. Williams, 1961; Searle, 1972; Bloch, 1975; and Eco, 1976).

Numerous elegant formulations have been spawned from these three perspectives, but surprisingly little progress has been made in understanding the society-culture relationships since the parameters of the problem were sketched by Karl Marx, Jacob Burckhardt, Alexis de Tocqueville, and Fustel de Coulanges well over a century ago.[4] In the absence of a demonstrable superiority of any one of the perspectives, debate has tended to polarize scholars into self-perpetuating schools in sociology along the materialist versus idealist lines of cleavage (Mullins, 1973).

Rather than enter the debate over differences, it seems strategic to ask what characteristics are *shared* by the three contending perspectives. There are three assumptions which may prove unnecessary. The first is that culture is a global and relatively coherent structure of symbols which (depending on one's perspective) is the social glue cementing social structure together, or it is a fog which provides the appearance of coherence while masking conflict and exploitation. The second common assumption is that substantive content of culture should be the focus of investigation.[5] The third common assumption is that culture changes only gradually and then by the unplanned process of accretion.[6]

## THE PRODUCTION PERSPECTIVE

The production-of-culture perspective neither denies the utility of these assumptions, nor denegrates studies made using them. Rather, it chooses the alternative tack of turning attention from the global corpus of habitual culture and focusing instead on the processes by which elements of culture are fabricated in those milieux where symbol-system production is most self-consciously the center of activity.[7]

As used here, the term "production" is meant in its generic sense to refer to the processes of creation, manufacture, marketing, distribution, exhibiting, inculcation, evaluation, and consumption. The first systematic research on the production of symbols in a single industry (in the United States, at least) was carried out by Robert Merton, Paul Lazarsfeld, and their associates at the Bureau of Applied Social Research following World War II. This line of research on mass media ground to a halt for a number of reasons by the mid 1950s (Wilensky, 1964; Jay, 1973; Gans, 1974; Peterson and DiMaggio, 1975).

Diverse studies of the immediate milieux in which elements of culture are produced have proliferated in the two decades since. The studies within each area are as diverse in intellectual orientation and methodology as the substantive foci are diverse. In consequence, there has been scant cumulative development. In sharp contrast to these exciting but scattered efforts, the sociology of science has moved ahead rapidly in recent decades. The progress has been made possible by turning away from grand questions about the relationship between science and society (cf. Merton, 1936), and focusing instead on the contexts in which science is made and remade (Hagstrom, 1965, 1976; Merton, 1973; Bourdieu, 1975; Ben-David and Sullivan, 1975). This rapid cumulative development in a sociology of science hints at the potential fruitfulness of a production process-oriented perspective.[8]

Drawing on the example of science, there seem to be three advantages in employing the production perspective. First, the scope of research is circumscribed enough in time and subject matter that small research projects can be cumulative. Second, concepts and methods developed in industrial, organizational, and occupational sociology as well as those employed in social psychology and economics can be borrowed.[9] Third, compari-sons across diverse areas will readily highlight communalities and parallels in the production of symbol systems. The search for communalities should not, however, be interpreted as a presumption that there are no consequential differences. On the contrary, as Crane (1976), Kadushin (1976), and Useem (1976) show, there are important differences between culture-producing milieux deriving from the ways they are socially structured and linked to society at large. This structuring is not inherent in the subject matter (cf. Becker, 1973; 1976) and is subject to quite remarkable variations over time.[10]

Perhaps the greatest shortcoming in the production perspective is that, while it is made to order for explicating the common mechanisms for making "normal culture"—to para-phrase Kuhn's (1970) term "normal science," it is ill-equipped to predict or even identify "cultural revolutions" in the making. Building on Kuhn, however, Heirich (1976) has suggested the conditions within which the regularly occurring fads in normal culture production are most likely to become revolutionary in scope. So that this initial search for communalities does not take us too far afield, the focus of the discussion which follows will be primarily on the three symbol-creating domains most often identified: art, science, and religion (cf. Parsons, 1961; Crane, 1972).

## INHIBITIONS AND OPPORTUNITIES

Two deep-seated habits of thought have inhibited the search for communalities in symbol production in art, science, and religion. The first is the belief that the three domains are essentially incompatible—that each follows a unique quest. A number of writers, for example, have asserted that while science advances, the arts follow a cycle of fashion. "Unlike the artist or author who has an infinite variety of paintings to paint, sculptures to sculpt or novels to write," Gaston (1973: 4) asserts, "the scientist has only one world to discover." This quest for a singular truth makes scientific communities different from those in the arts or religion, according to Price (1963) and Kuhn (1969, 1970: 160-173). But scientists are hardly the only ones to assert that they are on a unique quest. Theologians work within a specialized frame to more perfectly reveal God, while artists use shared techniques in search of Beauty beyond the realm of mundane experience.

If we find the occupational ideology of scientists more persuasive than these others, perhaps it is because we live in a highly rationalistic era. Whatever the case, it is counter-productive for us, as sociologists, to be drawn into a Kantian debate over "the reality of really real." As outside observers, we should treat such assertions of scientists, artists, and religionists as artifacts of occupational ideology, worthy of our investigation rather than our affirmation (Hughes, 1958: 42-50, 90-91; Thompson et al., 1969; Gusfield, 1976). A number of comparative research questions emerge when the assertions of a unique quest are taken as *social* fact rather than as *existential* fact. Several are suggested in the discussion which follows and in the other articles in this journal issue.

The assertion of unique quest has also served to inhibit comparative analysis *within* each of the three major domains. In part, the problem is like that of comparative anthropologists who must struggle to get beyond the assertion that traits of each society form a unique configuration and lose their meaning when abstracted from it. To be sure, it takes a great deal of time and effort to understand New York grand opera or Nashville grand ole opry. Nevertheless, it makes little sense to assert a priori that specific genres, fields, or faiths are unique and thus incomparable to others.

The second inhibition to the search for communalities is the assertion that high culture is more virtuous than low (or vice versa).[11] In each of the areas—art, science, and religion—the range of work contexts in which culture is produced can be viewed as a continuum from the pure, basic, theoretical, esoteric, or fine, to applied, practical, mundane, or popular. Since these terms are evaluatively loaded, the former sort will be called "academic" and the latter "commercial." While these terms, too, could be used normatively, they have the advantage of highlighting the *work context* in which culture is produced.

In the religious realm, researchers have contrasted the academic context where theology is created and modified with the competitive world of popular religion (Bellah, 1964; Heirich, 1974). In the arts, a cognate contrast has been drawn between the realm of academic fine arts and the world of mass-produced commercial art (Albrecht, 1973; Gans, 1974; Peterson, 1972a, 1975). The academic-commercial dimension does not *seem* to fit the case of science. As reflected in the sociology of science literature at least, all scientists appear to work in context at or near the "academic" end of the continuum. But if one looks at the production and dissemination of cognitive knowledge more broadly, it is apparent that the sociologists of science have focused on the elite academic end of a continuum which also includes, near the commercial end, engineering and popular science of diverse sorts which have received scant scholarly attention of the sort advocated here.[12] Even less systematic attention has been focused on that murky domain of discredited ideas where science, art, and religion meld (Bainbridge, 1973).

Notwithstanding its utility, the academic-commercial distinction itself has hindered comparative analysis. As Selznick and Selznick (1964), Nye (1970), and Gans (1974) have noted, researchers have all too often absorbed the self-serving ideological assertions of the academic culture-creators they study.

Academic practitioners often elevate their own activity by denigrating commercial culture as brutalizing, inauthentic, or mere entertainment. The impact of commercial forms on their consumers is a vital question, but too often a dehumanizing effect is *assumed,* and the study of popular culture itself is denigrated or dismissed as slumming. Such an elitist posture ill becomes the spiritual children of Francis Bacon.

Taken together, the two habits of thought just described, unique quest and false virtue, lead to a glorification of the creator and foster the simplistic view that the unique creative genius is always and everywhere threatened by the debasing demands of culture consumers (Morris, 1956; Becker, 1963; Guerard, 1969). This view systematically blinds the researcher to the complex mediating infrastructure between the two. It is perhaps the distinctive characteristic of the production-of-culture perspective that it focuses attention on this infrastructure.[1][3]

## MODES OF ANALYSIS

The production-of-culture perspective can be explored through either of two alternative modes of analysis, one synchronic and the other diachronic. Synchronic analysis involves the comparative study of the production process from creation to consumption. Of the numerous studies that have been made, those at the "academic" end of the range have focused primarily on the creation process, while most research on the "commercial" end has focused on the latter stages of the process. Among the numerous foci of inquiry in the synchronic mode of analyses, the following seem most important: the mechanisms by which "originality" and "innovation" are judged; the effects of different means of financing production (from patronage to market economy) on the sorts of symbols produced; the means of managing tensions of seeking esoteric group goals while being constrained by patrons and consumers to produce practical products; the impact of technology and the social organization of production on the kinds of symbols produced; the impact of "gatekeepers" (company executives, editorial boards, museums, ecumenical councils, censors, referees, accountants); the contexts in which culture products are used; and the impact of consumers on the production process.

The alternative mode of analysis is diachronic; here the effort is to find patterns in the ways in which culture forms change over time. Crane (1972: 129-142) has suggested that science, art, and religion each go through cycles of the sort described by Kuhn (1970) in which a phase of normal puzzle-solving within established paradigms alternates with revolutionary periods in which the paradigms themselves are altered. A second kind of cycle can be seen in each of the areas. Periods of purity (art, science, or theology for its own sake) alternate with periods when the social responsibility of culture producers is accentuated (Bensman and Gerver, 1958). Numerous other cyclical trends have been identified in the arts (Peterson, 1975). Are there comparable cycles in the other realms as well? To what extent are cycle phases in the different areas parallel in time? What sorts of forces propel the cycle, and to what extent are they internal to the realm or based in the environing society? Here again, the production-of-culture perspective opens up a world of interesting research questions.

## A GENETIC CONCEPTION OF CULTURE

The production perspective has been offered as a strategic retreat necessary to get around the difficult-to-research questions about the society-culture relationship. While research on the production of culture may strengthen one of the classical perspectives mentioned above, there is some indication that it will help to crystalize a new "genetic" perspective on the society-culture relationship. Talcott Parsons (1973) has offered the sketch for a genetic theory of culture, asserting that the "materialist" versus "idealist" debate which fueled so much sociological research over the past century has become increasingly sterile. He suggests that we turn our backs on such captivating classical questions as the association between protestantism and capitalism or the link between liberal democracy and an open class system. Drawing a parallel with developments in biology, he notes that the cognate "nature versus nurture" debate in biology was never resolved. Rather, it was supplanted by a detailed search for the genetic mechanisms such as DNA which, though trivial in their appearance, are the primary determinants of biological pattern and continuity. For these reasons, Parsons (1973: 45) suggests that mechanisms which create the pattern and form of society will be discovered by those of us working "in the human sciences dealing with cultural matters."

The orienting assumption of the genetic perspective is that culture is the code by which social structures reproduce themselves from day to day and generation to generation. In this view, culture plays the same role in sociology as genetics plays in biology.[14] The genetic perspective incorporates the commitments of the production perspective mentioned above, but it goes beyond the immediate milieux in which culture is deliberately produced as an end in itself to focus on those contexts where the culture code is inculcated[15] with or without deliberate modification.[16] The family, education, and media are clearly focal within this genetic perspective. Fully developed, it would cut across and suggest means of reintegrating most of the substantive sociologies of — noted at the outset.

This fresh look at the concept "culture" as "produced" and "genetic" is offered as a means of reinvigorating general sociology. The first fruits of this joint venture into cultural sociology are exemplified by, and cited in, the seven articles which follow.

## NOTES

1. A number of people were most helpful in nurturing the ideas reported here, and I would particularly like to thank Peter Blau, Alvin Gouldner, Robert Merton, Anthony Oberschall, Donald Ploch, Harrison White, and Mayer Zald. Funding for the Vanderbilt Symposium for which this paper was written was provided by grants from the National Science Foundation, Shell Foundation, and Vanderbilt University Research Council. Russell Davis, Patsy Doherty, and Betsy Schmidt have given unflagging assistance in producing the symposium and this special issue of the *American Behavioral Scientist*. Each of the symposium participants commented on

an earlier draft, and I would like particularly to thank the two discussants, Leo Lowenthal and Bernard Beck, for their incisive comments. In addition, Bernard Barber, Ivar Berg, Peter Berger, Pierre Bourdieu, Tom Burns, Priscilla Clark, Jerry Gaston, Thomas Gutterboch, Alex Inkeles, Rene Konig, Rosanne Martorella, John Meyer, Tim Patterson, Claire Peterson, Joachim Singelmann, Marcello Truzzi, and Barbara Walters made specific useful suggestions on at least one of the earlier drafts. Finally, I would like to acknowledge my debt to Paul DiMaggio, who has commented fruitfully from the earliest days of problem formulation to final editing.

2. In the final chapter of her study of invisible colleges of scientists, Diana Crane (1972) notes that there are numerous similarities in the production of science, art, and religion. Unhappy with the designation "sociology of knowledge," she proposes "sociology of culture" for this common field. The prime difference between her formulation and the one discussed here is that while she focusses on "high" science, art, and religion, we would incorporate the analysis of the production of "low" or popular culture in these three realms as well.

3. Of course it does violence to the ideas of many of the authors cited to place them exclusively in one or another of these orientations; think, for example, of David Riesman's (1950) *The Lonely Crowd*. Most would argue that all three have *some* utility, but the questions remain—where, when, and how?

4. A number of commentators have noted the lack of cumulative development in the sociology of culture (Duncan, 1968; Crane, 1972; Parsons, 1973; Geertz, 1973). While differing in other respects, each calls for a greater focus on the ways in which symbols are generated and changed.

5. Content can be focal for several quite different reasons. Symbolic artifacts may be analyzed to learn about the workings of social systems. This is the strategy of the structuralism developed by Levi-Strauss (Pettit, 1975). Alternatively, the content of culture may be prime grist for the sociologically informed critic of society (cf. Burns and Burns, 1973). Among American scholars at least, this tradition, which dates back to the debates over the efficacy and ethics of socialist realism, was put into eclipse in the 1950s by the paranoid excesses of McCarthyism. Yet today some critic-essayists including Susan Sontag, Irving Howe, Daniel Bell, Vincent Canby, and Tom Wolfe regularly use elements of culture to assay the condition of society in a way which research sociologists might find quite informative.

6. When symbol systems are deliberately fabricated or changed, they are usually labelled "ideology" and considered quite apart from culutre (Peterson, 1972b: 15-16).

7. It is noteworthy that those polemical opponents Mills (1959) and Parsons (1961) long since agreed that in complex industrial societies culture-symbol systems are increasingly produced in self-conscious, limited milieux.

8. As Michael Useem has noted in correspondence, this progress in the sociology of science has been bought at the price of accepting scientists' own definition of their domain as divorced from the rest of society, a focus which sets aside intriguing questions about the changing place of the scientific community in society. That this myopia is not *inherent* in the paradigm of culture production is suggested by his work (cf. Useem, 1976) as well as that of Bourdieu (1975), Hierich (1976), and others.

9. The focus on production should not obscure the fact that there is a difference between producing a refrigerator on the one hand, and a president, a play,

a law, a god, or a scientific formula on the other. In common these latter are invested with symbolic meaning well beyond their utility, and their creators are vested, in some degree, with "sacred" powers.

10. For example, contemporary American religious groups must compete for "consumers" in a free competitive market (Heirich, 1974), and their every assertion about the world is subject to the test of science. Science in turn is made by a self-perpetuating elite of esoteric specialists. Yet, the relative power position of these two systems of thought and the groups of persons who control them were very nearly just the opposite in Europe only 500 years ago. See also Kavolis (1974).

11. Highly educated and for the most part from the middle class, academics are thoroughly familiar with the high-culture critique of low culture. Because of their experience, however, they are less exposed to the inverse critique. In their review of the evidence on the injuries middle-class culture has had on the working class, Sennett and Cobb (1972) have not explicated the lower-culture critique of high culture. We are convinced, however, from work with the fans of country music, that there is a widely felt, if not clearly articulated, moralistic critique of high culture which is very nearly the same as the condemnation of low culture made by Haag and Rosenberg (Peterson and DiMaggio, 1975).

12. A most interesting example of the sorts of investigations possible in this area is provided by Kurt Back's (1972) study of the sensitivity training and encounter movement.

13. The research (cited in the references) made separately and in concert by Denisoff, Hirsch, DiMaggio, Berger, and Peterson has shown that even in the American commercial music industry, which is ostensibly devoted to giving the buying public exactly what it wants, the numerous elements of the infrastructure between creator and consumer significantly shape what the public gets. Similar findings seem to be emerging from a study of the quite different French recording industry being conducted by Jean-Pierre Vingolle and Antoine Hennion of the Ecole Nationale Superieure des Mines.

14. To date, what we know suggests that society is reproduced by amorphous mechanisms of a Lamarckian sort analogous to "acquired characteristics" in biology. Thus, it is unlikely that a mechanistic DNA of culture will soon be discovered.

15. Inculcation has a harsh sound but, it has the same place for society as socialization has for the individual.

16. No American general sociologist engaged in research today articulates this view, but just such a conception *is* fundamental to the broad range of linked empirical studies being carried out at the Center for European Sociology of the Sorbonne under the general direction of Pierre Bourdieu. Bourdieu often employs an economic metaphor in talking of cultural "stock," "capital," and "investments;" but he also speaks of culture as "reproducing" society in a way cognate with the genetic metaphor. The Bourdieu group has not published a fully developed statement of its perspective, but the range of its interests can be gauged by the projects described in "Current Research," published by the Center for European Sociology in 1972, and in its new journal, *Actes de la Recherche en Sciences Sociales.* The sophistication of this research is exemplified in Bourdieu (1968, 1973, 1974, 1975) Bourdieu and Darbel (1966) and Bourdieu and Passeron (1970).

# REFERENCES

ADORNO, T. W. (1968) Einleitung in die Musiksoziologie. Reinbek bei Hamberg: Rowohlt.
ALBRECHT, M. C. (1973) "The arts in market systems." Presented at the annual meeting of the American Sociological Association, New York.
BACK, K. W. (1972) Beyond Words: Sensitivity Training and The Encounter Movement. New York: Russell Sage.
BAINBRIDGE, W. (1973) "Deviant knowledge." M.A. Theory Paper in Sociology, Harvard University.
BECKER, H. S. (1976) "Art worlds and social types." Amer. Behav. Scientist 19 (July-August): 703-718.
––– (1973) "Art as collective action." Amer. Soc. Rev. 39 (December): 767-776.
––– (1963) Outsiders. New York: Free Press.
BELLAH, R. N. (1964) "Religious evolution." Amer. Soc. Rev. 29 (April): 358-374.
BEN-DAVID, J. and T. A. SULLIVAN (1975) "Sociology of science," pp. 203-222 in A. Inkeles (ed.) Annual Review of Sociology. Palo Alto, Calif.: Annual Reviews.
BENSMAN, J. and I. GERVER (1958) "Art and the mass society." Social Problems 6 (Summer): 4-10.
BERGER, P. (1963) "A market model for the analysis of ecumenicity." Social Research 30 (Spring): 77-93.
BLOCH, M. [ed.] (1975) Political Language and Oratory in Traditional Society. New York: Academic Press.
BLUMER, H. (1939) "Collective behavior," pp. 221-280 in R. E. Park (ed.) An Outline of the Principles of Sociology. New York: Barnes & Noble.
BORDIEU, P. (1975) "The specificity of the scientific field and the social conditions of the progress of reason." Social Sci. Information 14 (December): 19-47.
––– (1974) "Les fractions de la class dominante et les modes d'appropriation de l'oeuvre d'art." Social Sci. Information 13 (June): 7-32.
––– (1973) "Cultural reproduction and social reproduction," pp. 71-112 in R. Brown (ed.) Knowledge, Education, and Cultural Change. London: Tavistock.
––– (1968) Un Art Moyen. Paris: Les Editions de Minuit.
––– and A. DARBEL (1966) L'Amour de l'art: Les Musees d'art Europeens et Leur Public. Paris: Les Editions de Minuit.
BOURDIEU, P. and J. PASSERON (1970) La Reproduction. Paris: Les Editions de Minuit.
BURNS, E. and T. BURNS [eds.] (1973) Sociology of Literature and Drama. London: Penguin.
CRANE, D. (1976) "Reward systems in art, science and religion." Amer. Behav. Scientist 19 (July-August): 719-734.
––– (1972) Invisible Colleges: Diffusion of Knowledge in Scientific Communities. Chicago: Univ. of Chicago Press.
DENISOFF, R. S. (1975) Solid Gold. Rutgers, N.J.: Transaction Books.
––– and R. A. PETERSON [eds.] (1972) The Sounds of Social Change. Chicago: Rand-McNally.

DiMAGGIO, P. and P. M. HIRSCH (1976) "Production organizations in the arts." Amer. Behav. Scientist 19 (July-August): 735-752.

DUNCAN, H. D. (1968) Symbols in Society. New York: Oxford Univ. Press.

ECO, U. (1976) A Theory of Semiotics. Bloomington: Indiana Univ. Press.

GANS, H. J. (1974) Popular Culture and High Culture. New York: Basic Books.

––– (1957) "The creator-audience realtionship in the mass media: an analysis of movie-making," pp. 315-324 in B. Rosenberg and D. M. White (eds.) Mass Culture. New York: Free Press.

GASTON, J. (1973) Originality and Competition in Science. Chicago: Univ. of Chicago Press.

GEERTZ, C. (1973) The Interpretation of Cultures. New York: Basic Books.

GUERARD, A. L. (1969) Art for Art's Sake. New York: Schocken.

GUSFIELD, J. (1976) "The literary rhetoric of science." Amer. Soc. Rev. 41 (February): 16-33.

HAGSTROM, W. (1976) "The production of culture in science." Amer. Behav. Scientist 19 (July-August): 753-768.

––– (1965) The Scientific Community. New York: Basic Books.

HARAP, L. (1949) Social Roots of the Arts. New York: International Publishers.

HEIRICH, M. (1976) "Cultural breakthroughs." Amer. Behav. Scientist 19 (July-August): 685-702.

––– (1974) "The Sacred in a market economy." Presented at meeting of the American Sociological Association, Montreal.

HIRSCH, P. M. (1972) "Processing fads and fashions: an organization set analysis of cultural industry system." Amer. J. of Sociology 77 (January): 639-659.

––– (1969) The Structures of the Popular Music Industry. Ann Arbor: University of Michigan, Survey Research Center.

HUGHES, E.C. (1958) Men and their Work. New York: Free Press.

JAY, M. (1973) The Dialectical Imagination: A History of the Frankfurt School and the Institute of Social Research, 1923-1950. Boston: Little, Brown.

KADUSHIN, C. (1976) "Networks and circles in the production of culture." Amer. Behav. Scientist 19 (July-August): 769-784.

KAVOLIS, V. (1974) "Social and economic aspects of the arts," pp. 102-122 in Encyclopaedia Britannica (fifteenth ed.) Chicago: Encyclopaedia Britannica.

––– (1972) History on Art's Side. Ithaca, N. Y. Cornell Univ. Press.

––– (1968) Artistic Expression–A Sociological Analysis. Ithaca, N. Y.: Cornell Univ. Press.

KLAPP, O. E. (1969) Collective Search for Identity. New York: Holt, Rinehart & Winston.

KROEBER, A. L. (1957) Style and Civilizations. Berkeley: Univ. of California Press.

KUHN, T. S. (1970) The Structure of Scientific Revolutions. Chicago: Univ. of Chicago Press.

––– (1969) "Comment on the relations of science and art." Compar. Studies in Philosophy & History 11 (September): 403-412.

LOWENTHAL, L. (1964) "The reception of Dostoevski's work in Germany: 1880-1920," pp. 124-147 in R. N. Wilson (ed.) The Arts in Society. Englewood Cliffs, N.J.: Prentice-Hall.

––– (1961) Literature, Popular Culture, and Society. Englewood Cliffs, N.J.: Prentice-Hall.

MacDONALD, D. (1965) "Masscult and midcult," pp. 3-75 in Against the American Grain. New York: Vintage.

MERRILL, F. E. (1970) "Le Groupe des Batagnolles: a study in the sociology of art," pp. 250-259 in T. Shibutani (ed.) Human Nature and Collective Behavior. Englewood Cliffs, N.J.: Prentice-Hall.

MERTON, R. K. (1973) The Sociology of Science (N. Storer, ed.). Chicago: Univ. of Chicago Press.

——— (1936) "Puritanism, pietism, and science." Soc. Rev. 28 (September): 1-30.

MEYERSON, R. and E. KATZ (1957) "Notes on the natural history of fads." Amer. J. of Sociology 62 (May): 594-601.

MILLS, C. W. (1959) "The cultural apparatus." The (BBC) Listener 26 (March).

MORRIS, G.L.K. (1956) "Dilemmas of the modern artist: a comment." Art in America 44 (Fall): 41, 61-63.

MULLINS, N. C. (1973) Theories and Theory Groups in Contemporary American Sociology. New York: Harper & Row.

NYE, R. (1970) The Unembarrassed Muse. New York: Dial Press.

ORTEGA y GASSET, J. (1950) Revolt of the Masses. New York: New American Library.

PARSONS, T. (1973) "Culture and social structure revisited," pp. 33-46 in L. Schneider and C. Bonjean (eds.) The Idea of Culture in the Social Sciences. Cambridge: Cambridge Univ. Press.

——— (1961) "Culture in the social system," pp. 936-993 in T. Parsons et al. (eds.) Theories of Society, Vol. 2. New York: Free Press.

PETERSON, R. A. (1975) "Communalities in the production of high art and low: why cycles?" Social Theory and the Arts Conference, Fredonia, New York.

——— (1973) "The unnatural history of rock festivals: an instance of media facilitation." J. of Popular Music & Society 2 (Winter): 1-27.

——— (1972a) "A process model of the folk, pop, and fine art phases of jazz," pp. 135-151 in C. Nanry (ed.) American Music: From Storyville to Woodstock. New Brunswick, N.J.: Rutgers Univ. Press.

——— (1972b) The Industrial Order and Social Policy. Englewood Cliffs, N.J.: Prentice-Hall.

PETERSON, R. A. and D. G. BERGER (1975) "Cycles in symbol production: the case of popular music." Amer. Soc. Rev. 40 (April): 158-173.

——— (1971) "Entrepreneurship in organizations: evidence from the popular music industry." Administrative Sci. Q. 16 (March): 97-107.

PETERSON, R. A. and P. DiMAGGIO (1975) "From region to class, the changing locus of country music: a test of the massification hypothesis." Social Forces 53 (March): 497-506.

——— (1973) "The early Opry: its hillbilly image in fact and fancy." J. of Country Music 4 (Summer): 39-51.

PETTIT, P. (1975) The Concept of Structuralism: A Critical Analysis. Berkeley: Univ. of California Press.

PRICE, D. (1963) Little Science, Big Science. New York: Columbia Univ. Press.

RIESMAN, D. (1950) The Lonely Crowd. New Haven: Yale Univ. Press.

ROSENBERG, B. and D. M. WHITE [eds.] (1957) Mass Culture. New York: Free Press.

SAPIR, E. (1937) "Fashion," pp. 139-144 in Encyclopedia of the Social Sciences. New York: Macmillan.

SCHNEIDER, L. and C. BONJEAN [eds.] (1973) The Idea of Culture in the Social Sciences. Cambridge: Cambridge Univ. Press.

SEARLE, C. (1972) The Forsaken Lover: White Words and Black People. London: Routledge & Kegan Paul.

SELZNICK, G. J. and P. SELZNICK (1964) "A normative theory of culture." Amer. Soc. Rev. 29 (October): 653-669.

SENNETT, R. and J. COBB (1972) The Hidden Injuries of Class. New York: Vintage.

SOROKIN, P. (1937) Social and Cultural Dynamics. Vol. 1. New York: Bedminster.

THOMPSON, J. D., R. W. HAWKES, and R. W. AVERY (1969) "Truth strategies and university organization." Education Administration Q. (Spring): 5-25.

TYLOR, E. (1871) Primitive Culture. Gloucester, Maine: Smith.

USEEM, M. (1976) "Government patronage of science and art in America." Amer. Behav. Scientist 19 (July-August): 785-804.

WILENSKY, H. L. (1964) "Mass society and mass culture: interdependence or independence?" Amer. Soc. Rev. 29 (April): 173-197.

WILLIAMS, R. (1961) The Long Revolution. London: Chatto & Windus.

WOLFE, A. W. (1969) "Social structural bases of art." Current Anthropology 10 (February): 3-29.

*Recognizing that the production metaphor best fits the stages of normal culture production, Heirich shows how scientific, artistic, and religious modes of inquiry build upon societal roots to produce cultural breakthroughs of revolutionary character.*

# Cultural Breakthroughs

MAX HEIRICH
*University of Michigan*

**Thomas Kuhn,** the historian of science, distinguishes between what he calls "normal science" and "scientific revolutions." The first term refers to everyday science, which proceeds within commonly accepted paradigms or models that suggest what the universe is like, what questions are relevant to ask, and how one should gather evidence relating to these questions. In a revolution, Kuhn (1970) argues, the paradigm itself is changed so that quite different questions emerge, along with new procedures for answering them. Kuhn's distinction can be extended to cultural life more generally, to distinguish between those products that extend the understandings of their cultural world and those that fundamentally change the character of what appears later.

This paper focuses attention on changes of cultural perspective beyond the world of science. It will discuss the role a religious mode of inquiry plays in creating such "breakthrough" culture and will suggest social conditions conducive to the periodic intrusion of the religious mode into various areas of cultural life. The paper will contrast modes of inquiry with

**Author's Note:** *I wish to thank Richard Peterson and Barbara Walters for their thorough and perceptive responses to an earlier version of this presentation. They will recognize a number of places where their arguments have affected the contents of this paper.*

market modes for cultural production, noting not only the tension found between these approaches to the creation of culture, but also the ways they sometimes interact to produce a major shift in cultural understanding.

Although the culture worlds of art, science, and religion differ in the products they generate, certain modes of inquiry are found in all three. For convenience, I shall call these modes of inquiry artistic, scientific, and religious; each mode is named for the kind of product it most encourages. What I call the artistic mode of inquiry is found not only in the world of art but also in science and religion. Scientific and religious modes of inquiry also are found in all three culture worlds. But each mode of inquiry focuses attention on different things. It is these different foci for attention that most distinguish the products of each culture world.

## MODES OF INQUIRY

The artistic mode generates experiences that expand areas in which emotional reality can be shared rather than experienced in isolation. The artistic mode transforms human understanding by shifting our awareness of reality. In the field of art, the best products are approached as unique, one-of-a-kind experiences. This is partly an illusion, for artistic works of a particular time share understandings of reality that distinguish them from the products of another time period. Nonetheless, the essence of the artistic mode is the generation of experiences that touch their public deeply, that are experienced as unique, and that enlarge the range of what can be encountered collectively.

In contrast, the scientific mode of activity aims at simplifying the experience of reality by discovering principles of relationship that organize the complexity we see all around us. Careful attention to logical connections, to rules of verification and rejection, to the creation of emotional distance from the conclusions being considered, but not from the principles of inquiry being used, characterize the scientific mode. The task for the scientist is not the discovery of new areas of experience, but the organization of experience in terms of more abstract symbolic constructions.

The religious mode of cultural activity aims at discovering the ground of being from which other experiences of reality arise. It identifies the characteristics most important for coming to terms with that experienced reality and for transforming the self, so that one can relate to those principles that organize "real" (as contrasted with illusory) reality. This mode thus lies between the other two, partaking of elements of each of the others, but providing a focus that gives their activity quite different impact than they would have alone.

The religious mode does not necessarily require a conception of God or deities. Many of the more interesting religious responses today ignore such theological understandings, even as did such organized religions as Taoism or classic Buddhism. Indeed, both Paul Tillich and Peter Berger consider "non-sacred religion" to be the dominant form of religious understanding in the twentieth century (Tillich, 1959, 1969; Berger, 1969).

For most cultural production, the religious mode is not dominant. What might be called "normal culture" usually takes the commonly understood parameters for experiencing reality for granted, so that the ground of being in which events occur is not considered problematic. When the kind of breakthroughs in intellectual understanding occur that later get described as conceptual revolutions, however, the religious mode becomes far more central. Typically, they begin with a widening of experience (the artistic mode) that cannot be dealt with in terms of the normal framework for understanding reality. As the old frame dissolves, a new ground of being is asserted, whose dimensions become the parameters for organizing new experience. Within that new frame of reference, the simplifying sense of order that the scientific mode represents can then emerge.

**THE MARKET MODE OF PRODUCTION**

All three modes of inquiry that I have described assume that cultural products are valued in and of themselves, for the Truth they contain. In fact, however, cultural products often are produced for their exchange value as *commodities*. When the arrangements for funding cultural activity resemble those found in an economic market, "normal culture" subtly changes its character.

The dilemma of our time has been the degree to which the market mode has come to dominate all areas of cultural work. Most culture worlds (e.g., art, science, religion) develop a series of products that reflect the demands of their markets. Often this means that artistic, religious, or scientific conventions of style are used, independent of more fundamental modes of inquiry.

The vitality of cultural products does not depend upon their relation to "high" culture nor on the finesse with which they use the conventions of that culture world. (Consider, for example, the impact of Grandma Moses' painting.) Rather, vitality grows out of the seriousness with which the mode of inquiry is engaged.

## FADS AND BREAKTHROUGHS

All culture worlds seem susceptible to the emergence of intellectual fads—temporary bursts of excitement that seem to reorient the focus of activity, only to grow stale and be replaced by new enthusiasms. The difference between a fad and an intellectual breakthrough, I suspect, lies deeper than the question of whether or not culture producers remain committed to its perspective over time. Fads generate initial excitement by using a particular mode of inquiry in a fresh way. Usually, however, they do not reexamine the assumptions of "normal culture," but rather shift attention within the already accepted framework. Consequently, their repetition over time eventually loses its impact. In contrast, a cultural breakthrough changes some aspect of the framework that is used to experience reality and understand it. Extensions of that outlook, as a consequence, continue to generate excitement for long periods of time and can eventually redefine "normal culture" as the perspective becomes widely shared.

If I am correct in this basis for distinguishing between fads and breakthroughs, it follows that contemporaries should find it hard to distinguish between the two. Sometimes what appears to be a simple shift of emphasis actually changes the ground of being used to approach reality. Again, a dramatic shift of attention actually may leave the orienting framework undisturbed.

## THE EFFECTS OF DIFFERENT KINDS OF MARKETS

I am convinced that the nature of the markets for cultural products affects the ease with which potential "breakthrough" products can emerge. Moreover, markets affect the kind of following such a product is likely to have once it has appeared. As examples, let us compare consumer goods markets, those of organized religion, and those of academia which is the home of most theological production as well as the home of most innovative science.

As I see it, the most important difference in markets serviced by academia, by organized religion, and by consumer goods industries relates to how funds are acquired for the various enterprises. In America, organized religion is similar to consumer industries in depending for resources upon contributions raised from individual "consumers." This stems from a competitive, denominational form of religious organization, from constitutional prohibitions on state subsidy of religion, and from the geographical mobility of the population which makes it easy for many adherents to switch allegiances or to drop away completely.

This structural similarity in market conditions leads to a number of activities in the two spheres which are directly parallel. I have pointed elsewhere (Heirich, 1974) to similarities in product differentiation by demographic market, in range of sales techniques used, in oligopolistic organization of the religious market as well as of most consumers markets, to a tendency toward mergers, toward similar use of "trade associations," and toward similar criteria for the evaluation and promotion of personnel, based on management skills and on ability to increase income and membership. Just as in the case of consumer goods industries, the interplay of these factors makes for a succession of fads, not only in theology but also in the locus of sacred excitement for a larger public. Just as in the popular music industry, the length of the time that a sacred fad cycle remains dominant is about a decade (Heirich, 1974; Peterson, 1975).

Those parts of academia that are primarily teaching colleges and that depend upon individual tuition and fees (or upon legislative subsidy for teaching) reflect many of the characteristics just described. However, the more prestigious academic institutions (where the bulk of culturally innovative work that is shared beyond the immediate campus occurs) are dependent upon a different kind of market. They do not depend primarily on tuition or fees raised directly from individual consumers but on money from gifts, contracts, and grants.

Within prestigious universities, rewards are distributed on the basis of a star system, with "cultural innovators" eligible for star status, based upon a "publish or perish" tradition and review of performance by peers. Thus, individual access to rewards depends upon the opinion of colleagues both within and without one's own university. Institutional access to funds comes from a relatively small number of sources; the bulk of funds goes to units that are proven cultural innovators (i.e., to those who generate symbolic products that cause others to shift their way of thinking about the world and responding to it). Many of the funding sources are staffed by personnel who have themselves been academics; this is especially true of government grant agencies and private foundations. Thus, where religious innovators produce for a general public, academicians tend to produce for a relatively small set of peers, who control access to funds needed to carry on their activity.

The "publish or perish" tradition tends to generate high productivity; the star system encourages frequent new product designs within that production; and peer review, while it saves creative innovators from dependence upon the market as a whole, encourages the creation of products that are forward-looking, but not too far out of step with those that others are producing.

Not surprisingly, given all this, intellectual fads are as pervasive a feature of academic life as they are of organized religion. There tends to be a regular succession of "hot topics" in various fields and stylish new theoretical perspectives. What occur for the most part, are faddish shifts of emphasis that leave the dominant frameworks very much intact. Peer review, after all, encourages conceptualizations that are innovative but not too extreme. But the market for new intellectual products will promote conceptual revolutions, just as it will promote more conservative shifts of fad.

## GENERATING CONCEPTUAL REVOLUTIONS

Kuhn has relatively little to say about how conceptual revolutions are generated, other than to suggest that "normal science" gradually accumulates anomalies—findings that do not fit within the established paradigm. When enough of these accumulate, he suggests, people begin asking new questions that allow these findings to be taken into account. He does not try to explain the circumstances which allow anomalies to be taken seriously rather than dismissed—as, he contends, is the standard response within normal science. Nor does he identify the characteristics that make a new perspective revolutionary in its implications rather than merely different.

It seems to me that conceptual revolutions differ from intellectual fads in the following ways. First, they usually involve an experiential base that dissolves the *parameters* that have shaped previous ways of understanding events and meanings. Second, conceptual revolutions reorder the way parameters combine. Often only a single new ingredient is added, but it changes the values that each of the other concepts have, and consequently changes the organizing pattern for relationships that result when they interact.

Thus, the difference between intellectual fads and conceptual revolutions lies deeper than the simple question of how long enthusiasm for a new perspective lasts. A more fundamental distinction concerns the extent to which the new orientation taps what I have called the religious mode of symbolization. To the extent that the ground of reality is seen afresh, a conceptual revolution occurs.

I believe that the religious mode of inquiry is most likely to result in what we think of as a conceptual revolution when two circumstances are present. First, it arises in response to disorienting experiences that are widely shared by some relevant public. Second, it occurs in a context that provides a network of support for alternative perspectives.

What kinds of experiences allow a new sense of ultimate framework to emerge? The inevitability of organizing assumptions begins to dissolve for many observers when either of two situations occurs. First, if a large number of people begin to have experiences on a fairly regular basis that contradict what should be possible, it is only a matter of time until someone is likely to suggest a different set of organizing parameters for understanding these events. Second, fundamental reexamination of organizing perspectives also can be expected during time periods when quite undesirable outcomes seem to be imminent and unavoidable if reality operates in the ways one has previously assumed. These two situations are secularized statements of the classic view that religious response most often results either from mystical encounter (that shatters one's sense of the past and opens new possibilities for Reality) or from the experience of Judgment (when one is brought face to face with the consequences of living out of tune with an Ultimate sense of order).

**RECENT DEVELOPMENTS**

The Vietnam war, interestingly enough, seems to have created the circumstances in American intellectual circles, for both of these responses to emerge. In the mid-1960s the escalation of the war in Vietnam produced a strong protest movement in the United States, particularly among the generation tapped for direct participation in that venture. That protest centered on university campuses and produced some unexpected spin-offs.

First, the antiwar movement brought into question the rationality of government policy and priorities, among large numbers of intellectuals of all ages. Second, NDEA fellowship money, combined with widespread draft-dodging among young people unenthused about the war, diverted many of the best minds of a generation away from business and professional schools and into graduate academic training. Third, the protest movement led to the creation of a "counter-culture"—a deliberate effort among young radicals to establish a new way of life (often on the edge of university campuses) that would not perpetuate dominant American cultural practices. The counter-culture quickly absorbed energies that previously had gone into a range of less extreme social movements—including the civil rights efforts of the preceding decade, and the Peace Corps with its flock of disillusioned alumni who had tried to introduce "technological progress" in various parts of the world.

The counter-culture took advantage of new chemical products to reorient previous bases of relationships. Using newly developed contraceptive methods, they experimented with forms of sexual relationship and alternatives to the family as a basic unit of social life. And they began to use psychedelic chemicals and practices from eastern religions to shatter the limits of experienced reality. At first, it seemed as though the counter-culture was siphoning a portion of that generation out of serious involvement in the creation of cultural products for the larger society. Gradually it has become apparent, however, that it began to have impact not only on those who "dropped out" into it, but also on a much wider circle of young people in university communities and beyond.

Along with all this, an additional movement arose, sponsored in part by those who wished to redirect youthful energy away from "protest." The ecology movement began with encouragement from the political establishment as a concern to "clean up America." But it quickly joined forces with the war protest movement to focus attention on the "ecocide" in Southeast Asia, call attention to the role of American corporations in polluting the environment, and challenge the assumption that exponential technological growth was good—or possible over a very long period of time. Most important, the ecology movement began to question the fundamental assumption that humans were the center and controllers of the environment, stressing instead the symbiotic relationships among species and limits to human independent action.

As these styles of thought began to take root among academics, the larger consequences of the Vietnam war began to be visible as well. American dominance began to be seriously challenged, not only militarily but also financially, because of the weakened position of the American dollar in the world economy. The emergence of new coalitions of nations that controlled vital resources and the proliferation of nuclear technology among less technologically developed countries harbingered a more fundamental shift of power based on the capacity to inflict terror on others.

These shifts in the objective position of the nation began to occupy the attention of scholars of all ages, even as the war-generated movements among college-age youth provided new foci for questions. Numerous groups have emerged seeking new meaning for this shattered world (and world view). Included here are groups within the natural and social sciences that make sufficiently distinct assumptions about the basis of reality to be contenders for the status of new paradigm-creators. Two of these, the "futurists" and the "counter-culture physicists," will be examined in some detail. It is much too early to judge, but they offer promise of being more than intellectual fads; and they seem to suggest fundamentally different orientations to the intellectual issues they confront.

**Example 1: The Futurists
("Secular Judgment")**

In the last few years a spate of writings has emerged among social and physical scientists assessing the human prospect. One thinks, for example, of such writers as Robert Heilbroner (1974), Barrington Moore (1972), Buckminster Fuller (1970, 1972, 1973), the group calling themselves the Club of Rome (Meadows et al., 1972), scientists like Dennis Pirages and Paul Erlich (1974), the historian Charles Bright (1975), and others who have extended the assessment of technological society begun ten years ago by Herbert Marcuse (1964). These writers call into question the technological base of current social organization and warn of its imminent collapse. Their prophetic writing can best be described as "secular Judgment." The Futurists, as this "fad" has come to be called, present a modern version of the Fall of Man—a sense that human striving has come to challenge the fundamental order of the universe and is beginning to falter before it.

The Futurists posit an ecological system which effectively limits the range of activities that humans can impose on the world. Many see industrial expansion at its present exponential growth rates ending within the next fifty years, due to limitations on natural resources and energy supplies needed to sustain such activity. And most see the emergence of "no-growth economies" as requiring fundamental change in the way human beings relate to one another, both *within* advanced industrial nations that heve depended on industrial expansion for their prosperity, and *between* nations. Their ecological perspective removes humans from the center of the universe, having dominant control over it through science and technology.

Some of these social prophets shift the ground of reality still more radically, relating shifts in bases of dominance and control to the coming necessity of no-growth economies. The historian Charles Bright (1975), for example, forecasts an upswing in political repression ' within advanced industrial nations as no-growth economies emerge: such developments make unworkable the formula by which class struggles over distribution of wealth have been contained in advanced industrial nations over the past eighty years. No longer will exponential growth rates for the economy permit escalation of wages and an expanding tax base for the welfare state, both of which have served to "buy off" worker discontent. More direct repression of dissent is likely as a consequence, he argues.

More importantly, according to Bright, this exponential growth formula cannot be extended to the currently under-developed nations, because of resource limitations. Yet they are just now emerging as politically independent, effectively organized areas, with control over key resources, and some now possess nuclear weapons; they are increasingly capable of demanding their share of world wealth.

Thus, argues Bright, we are likely to enter a period of increasing chaos in the next few decades, with nation states unable to deal with the fundamental struggles over resources that emerge, and with the combined ecological limits and "international class struggle" gradually forcing a rethinking of technology and of the kind of science-based relationship patterns that have characterized the modern era. The apocalyptic social forecasters vary in the degree to which they share this sense of the total dissolution of frameworks for orienting social activity. But all of these intellectuals begin with a new sense of where the ground of reality lies—one that requires fundamental transformation of human responses.

### Example 2: Counter-Culture Physicists ("Secular Mysticism")

One of the most interesting cultural developments within the last three years has been the emergence of a group of scientists who describe themselves as "counter-culture physicists." In terms of conventional science, they are involved in extending and formalizing the kinds of theories represented by Einstein's theory of relativity. Their focus, however, is upon *conscious-*

*ness,* an area about which conventional science, heretofore, has had little to say (Kauffmann, 1973). It is not unusual for individual physicists to engage in metaphysical speculation, but it *is* unusual for a network of physicists to focus on questions of this sort as their shared scientific pursuit. Some of them describe the major intellectual task of the next few decades as being that of bringing into one coherent framework insights from science and religion.

As their label for themselves implies, these intellectuals trace the roots of their current inquiry to experiences generated by explorations of the counter-culture. These scholars play the conventional games of academia insofar as normal culture production is concerned. They publish theoretical papers in the standard journals, attend international symposia, seek foundation funds, and establish their credentials as technically competent "producers." But the questions they ask, while discussible within the language of ordinary science, do not grow primarily out of that tradition. They stem from experiences that a few years ago would simply have served to label the participants as mentally deranged (cf. Finkelstein, 1972; Taylor, 1974).

As I see it, the task these younger intellectuals have set for themselves is very much akin to tasks undertaken by many of the best cultural producers in the field of religion. They seem to have begun with their own experience of nonordinary reality. This has included "energy flows" experienced directly between people; unusual experiences of time and space; experiences or observation of precognition, telepathy, clairvoyance, and/or psychokinesis; and shatteringly new senses of how organic and inorganic life are related through time and space. These experiences amount not to a shift of emphasis, but to a virtual dissolution of the ways that time, space, energy, light, matter, organic and inorganic life are assumed to interrelate. Because there was a network of people having similar experiences of this kind, both with and without the aid of drugs, the experiences were accepted as real and as requiring a reformulation of physical principles used to understand experience.

This, of course, is not the first time that physical scientists have explored these areas. Heisenberg's explorations of yoga

(1971), Einstein's mystic interests (1972), Madame Curie's efforts to communicate with her deceased husband (1974), and the long line of distinguished scientists who have headed British organizations for the study of psychic phenomena attest to an on-going mystical streak within the scientific community. What is different this time is the emergence of a network of scientists taking these kinds of questions not as their focus for scientific *observation,* but as the orienting perspective for formulating theoretical issues of more general application. They have a journal *(Foundations of Physics)* and contribute widely to other publications as well, with questions chosen in terms of their relevance to this quest, whether or not other readers recognize the thrust.

For the past few years, theoretical physicists (of both "straight" and "counter-culture" perspectives) have been trying to create a formal statement of theories of gravity, of which Einstein's general relativity theory would be the best known, but not the only version (cf. Will, 1974). The most influential of the recent formulations are what are called metric theories of gravity. These assume that gravitation can be treated as synonymous with the curvature of time and space. This means that all physical systems behave as though the events were taking place in non-Euclidean space-time.

The counter-culture physicists have taken this work a step further. They suggest that negative mass contributes to the geometric shape of space by screening gravitational waves, so that a variety of gravitational fields results (cf. Sciama, 1974; Sarfatti, 1974b). If this is so, each field may be responsible for a particular scale of organization of matter, including biogravitons that organize living systems. With the coexistence of various kinds of gravitational fields, many current understandings of causality principles shift. Time, for example, flows in two directions; space continues to vary by its relation to gravity fields, as Einstein noted, but there are many more possibilities for interconnection in space than seemed true before, including connections between various layers of reality. Thus, causality may flow from the mind and consciousness as well as in the other direction. And various combinations of gravitational fields should allow interactions that seem to contradict our present understanding of physical principles. Such "altered states of consciousness" as telepathy, precognition, and even psycho-kinesis and astral projection become describable in terms of the principles of physics (Walker, 1970; Scarfatti, 1974a).

If this effort to extend general relativity theory in directions that can deal with *consciousness* is successful, it will reorient many of the questions asked in various intellectual fields—in psychology, physics, philosophy, and religion at the very least. Thus, it potentially dissolves not only the conceptual frame-work that constricted thought in the past, but also the organizational boundaries that limit *who* will exchange ideas.

### MARKETING REVOLUTION

In these two examples, we see how secularly produced encounter can lead to conceptual breakthroughs that are religious in quality and that dissolve the hold of the past on ways of seeing, experiencing, and organizing understandings. Earlier I suggested that the market mode within which most intellectual activity is pursued in America coopts and trivializes the revolutionary quality of new formulations so that their impact is diminished. But there are some circumstances under which this method of promotion may actually increase the impact, rather than destroy it.

Packaging ideas as commodities, to be pushed in the same manner that other commodities are, lessens the impact they can make over time—unless that impact depends in part on scale of exposure or on linking specialists who are isolated by conventional disciplinary boundaries. In such cases, the market mode's capacity for promoting symbols as fad items may facilitate the process of new paradigm formation just as, in the quest after profits, mass media corporations disseminated the ethos of the 1960s youth culture (Peterson, 1973).

Three specific examples of how the marketing mode has helped to facilitate the development of counter-culture physics and apocalyptic forecasting come to mind. First, a popular paperback book, *Psychic Discoveries Behind the Iron Curtain,* written in laymen's language by two journalists (Ostrander and Schroeder, 1970), seems to have alerted scientists from many disciplines to areas of common researchable questions that deal with the interaction of consciousness and physical events. Second, a few of the counter-culture physicists have attempted a similar breakthrough of communication, collaborating with an artist-illustrator to produce a cartoon-like exposition of their ideas, with notes alerting the reader to brief summaries of current arguments in general relativity theory and to an annotated bibliography to allow interested readers to delve more deeply (Toben et al., 1975). Third, the apocalyptic forecasters also have written for a general intellectual audience, eschewing technical language and arguments that would limit the audience for their presentation (cf. Pirages and Erlich, 1974).

It is too early to judge the fate of the two cultural breakthroughs just described. They make it clear, however, that the religious mode of inquiry continues to thrive and even uses the market mode to spread its message.

Sometimes cultural breakthroughs lead to conceptual revolutions for a large number of culture consumers; at other times they result simply in the creation of a deviant cult, which sees things differently from the mainstream of humanity, but which has little impact on the way others understand the world. Which result occurs probably depends on three factors: on the social conditions that prevail after the reformulation has been made and that affect receptivity to the new outlook; on the ability of the perspective to produce new insights beyond those which gave it its origin; and on the ability of the new outlook to gain sponsors among gatekeepers to facilities for the dissemination of cultural products.

This paper started from Kuhn's description of conditions for a scientific revolution and has extended the perspective to describe cultural activity more generally. In doing so, it has focused on how modes of inquiry differ, how they nonetheless are found across many fields of cultural work, and how "normal cultural production" uses a market mode that changes the character of what is produced. I have argued that conceptual revolutions are based upon a religious mode of inquiry which becomes activated when disruptions occur in the social experience of culture-producing communities. Once generated, such a revolution must be able to incorporate the artistic and scientific modes as well in order to succeed: it must produce experiences that emotionally validate this sense of reality, while clarifying conceptions of how parts of the world relate to one another. The argument has closed by coming full circle once again to Kuhn, offering a more general statement of his argument about conditions affecting the establishment of new paradigms once they emerge.

Revolutions in cultural understandings do not result simply from particular modes of inquiry, from market conditions for the dissemination of ideas, or from shifts in social circumstance for producers of culture alone. Together, however, these factors make possible the kinds of cultural breakthroughs that have revolutionary impact, in which the world is seen anew.

## REFERENCES

BERGER, P. (1969) Sacred Canopy. New York: Doubleday.

BRIGHT, C. (1975) Unpublished manuscripts. University of Michigan, Department of History.

CURIE, M. S. (1974) Correspondence: choix de lettres 1905-1934. Paris: Editeurs francais reunis.

EINSTEIN, A. (1972) Correspondence, 1903-1955. Paris: Hermann.

FINKELSTEIN, D. (1972) "The space-time code." Physical Rev. 5D, 12 (June 15): 2922.

FULLER, R. B. (1973) Earth, Inc. New York: Doubleday.

——— (1972) Utopia or Oblivion: The Prospects for Humanity. New York: Overlook.

——— (1970) Operating Manual for Spaceship Earth. New York: Touchstone Clarion.

HEILBRONER, R. (1974) An Inquiry into the Human Prospect. New York: Norton.

HEIRICH, M. (1974) "The sacred as a market economy." Presented at the annual meeting of the American Sociological Association, Montreal.

HEISENBERG, W. (1971) Physics and Beyond. New York: Harper & Row.

KAUFFMANN, W. J. III (1973) Relativity and Cosmology. New York: Harper & Row.

KUHN, T. (1970) The Structure of Scientific Revolutions. Chicago: Univ. of Chicago Press.

MARCUSE, H. (1964) One Dimensional Man. Boston: Beacon.

MEADOWS, D. H., D. L. MEADOWS, J. RANDERS, and W. W. BEHRENS III (1972) The Limits to Growth: A Report from the Club of Rome's Project on the Predicament of Mankind. New York: Universe.

MOORE, B. (1972) Reflections on the Causes of Human Misery and Certain Proposals to Eliminate Them. Boston: Beacon.

OSTRANDER, S. and L. SCHROEDER (1970) Psychic Discoveries Behind the Iron Curtain. Englewood Cliffs, N.J.: Prentice-Hall.

PETERSON, R. A. (1975) "Communalities in the production of high art and low: why cycles?" Social Theory and the Arts Conference, Fredonia, New York.

——— (1973) "The unnatural history of rock festivals: an instance of media facilitation." J. of Popular Music & Society 2: 1-27.

PIRAGES, D. C. and P. R. ERLICH (1974) Ark II: Social Response to Environmental Imperatives. New York: Viking.

SARFATTI, J. (1974a) "Implications of meta-physics for psychoenergetic systems," Psychoenergetic Systems, Vol. 1. London: Gordon & Breach.

——— (1974b) "The eightfold way as a consequence of the general theory of relativity." Collective Phenomena 1.

SCIAMA, D. W. (1974) "Gravitational waves and Mach's principle." Trieste, Italy: International Center for Theoretical Physics, Reprint 1C/73/94.

STAPP, H. P. (1971) "S-Matrix interpretation of quantum theory." Physical Review D3: 1303.

STEIGMAN, G. (1974) "Antimatter in the universe." Int. Rep. IC/73/110. International Center for Theoretical Physics, Trieste, Italy.

TAYLOR, J. G. (1974) Black Holes: The End of the Universe? New York: Random House.

TILLICH, P. (1969) What is Religion? New York: Harper & Row.

——— (1959) Theology of Culture. New York: Oxford Univ. Press.

TOBEN, B., J. SARFATTI, and F. WOLF (1975) Space, Time and Beyond. New York: E. P. Dutton.

WALKER, E. H. (1970) "The nature of consciousness." Math. Biosciences 7: 138-178.

WILL, C. M. (1974) "Gravitational theory." Scientific Amer. (November): 25-33.

*Becker contrasts the work worlds of integrated professionals, mavericks, naive artists, and folk artists.*

# Art Worlds and Social Types

HOWARD S. BECKER
*Northwestern University*

**Define a world** as consisting of all those people and organizations whose activity is necessary to produce the kind of events and objects which that world characteristically produces. Then an art world consists of the people and organizations who produce those events and objects that world defines as art. Let me explicate the tautology and in so doing indicate four uses it has in comparative research. The definition suggests the following propositions and questions.

(1) Works of art can be understood by viewing them as the result of the coordinated activities of all the people whose cooperation is necessary in order that the work should occur as it does. This sets a distinctive agenda for our inquiry. We are to look, first, for the complete roster of kinds of people whose activity contributes to the result. As I have suggested elsewhere (Becker, 1974), this might include people who conceive the idea of the work (e.g., composers or playwrights); people who execute it (musicians or actors); people who provide the necessary equipment and materials (e.g., musical instrument makers); and people who make up the audience for the work

(playgoers, critics, and so on). Although we conventionally select some one or a few of these as "the artist" to whom responsibility for the work is attributed, it is sociologically more sensible and useful to see the work as the joint creation of all these people.

(2) The definition makes problematic the coordination of the activities of all these people. The solution to the problem which furnishes the best possibility of uniting the work of humanists and social scientists is that people coordinate their activities by reference to a body of conventional understandings embodied in common practice and in the artifacts of the world (Gombrich, 1960; Meyer, 1956; Smith, 1968). The notion of conventions, while intuitively understandable, needs more analysis. Here it is sufficient to say that conventions make possible the cooperative activities through which the world's products come about, and make them possible with a relatively low investment of time and energy.

(3) Common usage so strongly suggests that there will, at any time, be only one art world that it is necessary to insist on the most circular element in the definition: that a world consists of those whose activity is essential to produce whatever they produce. In other words, we do not start by defining art and then looking for the people who produce the objects we have thus isolated. Instead, we look for groups of people who cooperate to produce things that they, at least, call art; having found them, we look for all the other people who are also necessary to that production, gradually building up as complete a picture as we can of the entire cooperating network that radiates out from the works in question. Thus, it is perfectly possible, theoretically and empirically, for there to be a great many such worlds coexisting at one time. They may be unaware of each other, in conflict, or in some sort of symbiotic or cooperative relation. They may be relatively stable, the same people continuing to cooperate in much the same way over some period of time, or quite ephemeral, coming together only on the one occasion when they produce a particular work. People may participate in only one world or in a large number,

either simultaneously or serially. Only aesthetic or philosophical prejudice, not any scientific necessity, requires us to choose one of the existing worlds as authentic and dismiss the others as less important or less than the real thing.

(4) An organized world is the source of whatever social value is ascribed to a work (Danto, 1964; Dickie, 1971; Levine, 1972). The interaction of all the involved parties produces a shared sense of the worth of what they collectively produce. Their mutual appreciation of the conventions they share and the support they mutually afford one another convinces them that what they are doing is worth doing, that the products of their effort are valid works.

## TYPES OF ARTISTS

We can describe participants in worlds with reference to the degree to which they participate in or depend on the regularities of behavior of which the collective action of the world consists and on which its results depend. I will focus on those participants who are ordinarily and officially viewed as "artists" (in the ideologies of their respective worlds). In principle, the same sort of description could be given of other participants in these systems of collective action. Let us begin by considering some common-sense, empirically recognizable types of artists, seeing what understanding we can gain of their work by placing them in the context of worlds and conventions just described.

### Integrated Professionals

Imagine, for any particular organized art world, a canonical art work, a work done exactly as the conventions current in that world dictate. A canonical art work would be one for whose doing all the materials, instruments, and facilities have been exactly prepared. It would be a work of art for whose doing every cooperating person—performers, providers of supplies, support personnel of all kinds, and especially audiences—

have been exactly trained. Such a work could be created with a minimum of difficulty, since everyone involved would know exactly what to do. People would provide the proper materials, performers would know just how to interpret the directions given them, museums would have exactly the right kind of space and lighting for the work to appear in, audiences would be able to respond with no difficulty to the emotional experiences the art work created, and so on. Such a work might, of course, be relatively dull for everyone involved, since by definition it would contain nothing novel, unique, or attention-getting. Nothing would violate expectations. Thus, no tension would be created and no emotion aroused. An extreme, a caricature, of such a work might be the background music played in restaurants or the paintings one finds on motel walls.

Envision, too, a canonical artist, an artist fully prepared to produce, and fully capable of producing, the canonical art work. Such an artist would be fully integrated into the art world as it is. He would cause no trouble for anyone who had to cooperate with him, and all his works would find a large and responsive audience. We might call him an "integrated profes-sional" (Blizek, 1974).

In any organized art world, of necessity, most of the artists will be integrated professionals. Because they know, under-stand, and habitually use the conventions on which their world runs, they fit easily into all the standard activities that world carries on. If they are composers, they write music performers can read and play on available instruments; if they are painters, they use available materials to produce works which, in size, form, design, color, and content, "fit" into the available spaces and into people's ability to respond appropriately. They stay within the bounds of what potential audiences and the state consider respectable. Such regular ways of doing things cover every aspect of the production of art works: materials, forms, contents, modes of presentation, sizes, shapes, durations, and modes of financing. In using and conforming to the conventions in these matters, integrated professionals make it possible for art works to be made relatively efficiently and easily. Coordination of the activities of large numbers of people can occur with a minimum investment of time and energy, simply by identifying the conventions everyone should follow.

Everyone in an art world would, all other things equal, prefer to deal with integrated professionals. It makes life much easier. But everyone connected with an art world also expects that world not to produce exactly the same work over and over, but to produce at least variations and innovations, even though the differences may actually be quite small between successive works. A fully professionalized art world may become enslaved by the conventions through which it exists, producing what we would call (if we take the results seriously) hack work. Most members of any art world are probably considered, and consider themselves, hacks, though they might prefer to use terms like "competent professional," "journeyman," and the like. The academic painter, at the height of his academy's ascendancy, exemplified the type, as did the successful playwright in Broadway's heyday during the 1930s. White and White (1965) discuss just such people in their analysis of French painting, reminding us that the bulk of professional painters in the nineteenth century were completely oriented to what they nicely term the "art machine" of the time.

Those artists who are seen by members of the world as more creative, those who produce the marginal variations and innovations which ·do not violate convention sufficiently to disrupt coordinated actions, are, of course, not called hacks. Whatever the positive term used in their world, we might perhpas best think of them as contemporary stars. This suggests the general point that each of the types we will discuss contains examples both of artists and work regarded as unoriginal and worthless and of artists and work regarded as first-rate.

In emphasizing the relative ease with which integrated professionals get work done, I do not mean to suggest that they never have any trouble. Though the participants in an art world have a common interest in getting things done, they also have private interests which often conflict. Many conflicts arise between different categories of participants and are, in fact, chronic and traditional. Playwrights and composers want their works performed as they envision them. But actors and musicians like to perform those works so that they show themselves off to best advantage. Authors would like to revise their novels right through the stage of page proofs, but that costs more money than publishers like to invest. The diaries and letters of artists are filled with complaints over the intransigence of those they work with and with accounts of bitter struggles over such points.

## Mavericks

Every organized art world produces mavericks. Mavericks are artists who have been part of the conventional art world of their time, place, and medium, but who found it unacceptably constraining, to the point where they were no longer willing to conform to its conventions. Where the integrated professional accepts almost completely the conventions of his world, the maverick retains some loose connection to that world but refuses to conform, thus making it impossible for himself to participate in the world's organized activities.

Not surprisingly, mavericks experience grave difficulties in getting their work done. Sometimes the difficulties are so great that the work cannot be realized, only planned. For example, much of Charles Ives' work received no real performances during his working lifetime (Cowell and Cowell, 1954; Perlis, 1974). If the works are realized, the maverick accomplishes this only by ignoring the established institutions of the art—the museums, concert halls, publishers, theaters—and establishing his own. Writers print and distribute their own work. Visual artists devise works which cannot be exhibited in museums—earth works, conceptual art—thus escaping what they feel to be the tyranny of museum directors and financial supporters. Actors, playwrights, and directors develop street theater forms. Artists in general recruit followers, disciples, and helpers, often from the ranks of the untrained and the unprofessional, and create their own network of cooperating personnel, even to the point of recruiting new audiences.

Even so, mavericks have come from an art world, were trained in it, and remain to some important degree oriented to it. That is evident in the selectivity with which they deal with existing conventions. It seems that the maverick's intention is to force recognition from that world, requiring it to adapt to the conventions the maverick has established as the basis of his work rather than him adapting to theirs. For mavericks do not renounce all, or even very many, of the conventions of their art. If James Joyce was iconoclastic with respect to literary and even linguistic forms of his day, he still wrote a finished book. He did not, for instance, write a work like Joe Gould's *History of the World,* which among other things would never be finished and not all of which may have been written down (Mitchell, 1965); nor did he devise a literary form that would be chanted instead of being printed or one in which his own personal calligraphy would be an important element of his composition. He wrote a perfectly recognizable European book. Similarly, creators of earth works are, after all, creating sculpture; the materials, the scale, and the setting of their works are unconventional, but the concerns with form and volume are shared with more canonical sculptors.

Ives had such innovative notions of melody, tonality, and performance standards that contemporary musicians could not or would not play his work, and audiences did not like the little of it they heard. Yet Ives wrote for conventional instruments; he used normal forms of instrumentation and normal musical forms (the sonata, symphony, and artsong). John Cage and Harry Partsch went much farther than Ives in challenging conventional musical organization.[1] Cage used specially pre-pared instruments, while Partsch (1949) required that special instruments be built to play his music. They both (and, of course, they are not alone in this) require that performers learn to interpret a new musical notation in order to play what they have written. Cage goes even further than Partsch in requiring that the performer contribute much more to the determination of what notes will be played and what sounds will be made. While conventional composed music leaves little leeway for the performer in this respect, Cage's instructions are often mere sketches, and the performer must fill out the specific notes and rhythms. For all of these innovations, however, both Cage and Partsch still rely on the notion of the concert as the chief way to present their works to a public. People still buy tickets, file into a hall at an appointed time, and sit quietly while a performance is put on for them.

In short, the maverick orients himself to the world of canonical and conventional art. He puts his mind to changing some of the conventions of its operation and more or less unwittingly accepts all the rest. The work of these innovators often ends up being totally incorporated into the historical corpus of the production of that established art world. People in that world find the innovations useful in producing the variation required to rescue art from ritual. Innovations become more acceptable through familiarity and association. Their essential fit with all the other conventions makes it relatively easy to assimilate them. Mavericks deal with the same people who manufacture the material used by more conventional artists, but demand new things of them, as they do of the support personnel others rely on. They look to be supported and appreciated by the same audiences more conventional artists work for, although they demand more work from audiences by virtue of the increased difficulty of responding to the new and unfamiliar works.

Because maverick work shares so much with conventional work, we can see the more general point that maverickness is not an inherent characteristic of a work, but rather is to be found in the relation between the work and the conventional art world to which it is related. Maverick work chooses to be difficult for that world to assimilate, a difficulty that world refuses to take on, at least for a while. If the contemporary art world does adapt, then the artist and the work lose their maverick quality, since the conventions of the world encompass what was once foreign. Because the maverick becomes the conventional, and not just because life offers us many intermediate cases, it is hard to draw a line between the innovating integrated professional and the maverick.

Just as not all the work of integrated professionals is thought to be of high quality, so very few mavericks gain the respect of the art world they are quarrelling with. In fact, most participants in that world probably never hear of the vast majority of mavericks, and very few of those who are heard of end up being thought well of. Instead, they remain curiosities whose work may be revived from time to time by interested antiquarians or stimulate the imagination of newcomers. An interesting musical example is the work of Conlon Nancarrow, who creates music for player piano by the unconventional method of punching holes directly into the piano roll.[2] He can thus produce effects such as the chromatic glissando, otherwise unobtainable on the piano and has used these possibilities to create some enormously interesting and moving music. But the innovation has never caught on, and those musicians aware of his work regard it as little more than an interesting curiosity.

## Naive Artists

A third kind of artist, one receiving considerable attention in the visual arts now, is alternately called "primitive," "naive," or "grass-roots." Grandma Moses is the prototype, although she eventually was discovered by the art world and enjoyed quite a vogue (not an uncommon experience for such people). These artists will very likely have had no connection with any art world at all. They do not know the members of the ordinary art world in which works like theirs are produced. They have not had the training that people who ordinarily produce such works have had; and they know very little about the nature of the medium they are working in, its history, conventions, or the kind of work ordinarily produced in that medium. Unable to explain what they do in conventional terms, naive artists typically work alone, for no one else knows how to do what they need done by way of assistance or cooperation, and no language exists in which to explain it. Insofar as they do have help, they must create their own network of cooperation—

recruiting, training, and maintaining a group of people who gradually learn what is needed and how to do it. Most frequently, they succeed at best in recruiting some few people to play the role of appreciators of the work.

I have made the work seem more conventional than it is by suggesting that it fits into such standard categories as painting or musical composition. Often enough it does; Grandma Moses is only one of a large number of primitive painters, whose most famous exemplar is Henri Rousseau. These people know and abide by the conventions of easel painting, painting on conventional-sized canvasses or boards with more or less conventional materials (Bihalji-Merin, 1971).

Many naive artists go far beyond that. Think of Simon Rodia, the man who built the Watts Towers in Los Angeles (Trillin, 1965). The Towers are certainly too enormous a project to be called sculpture yet one would not exactly think of them as architecture either. They consist of several open-work towers, made of reinforced concrete, the tallest over 100 feet. Rodia decorated the towers with a variety of easily available materials: pop bottles, dime store crockery, and so on. He made impressions in the cement with all kinds of kitchen utensils, craftsmen's tools, and so on. He relied on the skills he learned as a tile setter, and his imagery is quite idiosyncratic, although probably more religious than anything else. In any event, the Watts Towers stand as the sole member of their class; there is no other work like them. And that uniqueness suggests what is true—that Rodia, like other naive artists, operated totally outside the conventional cooperative networks which characterize the arts.

Naive artists achieve their idiosyncratic style and create forms and genres which are unique and peculiar because they have never acquired and internalized the habits of vision and thought the professional artist necessarily acquires in the course of training. A maverick has to fight clear of the habits left by professional training, but the naive artist has never had them. Many of the artists who make constructions requiring the kinds of skills the Watts Towers demanded got their skills as Rodia did, as members of one or another of the building trades. Others have been farmers or general handymen. To put it more generally, societies teach many people numerous skills which can be put to artistic use, but teach them in nonartistic settings and for utilitarian purposes. People who have acquired these skills can then set out on idiosyncratic art enterprises without ever having come in contact with the conventional art world. This may explain why it is hard to find musical examples to parallel the visual ones; it is relatively unusual for people to acquire musical skills in that casual and unprofessional way, because musical skills are so specialized that they are not useful in nonartistic enterprises.

Having had no professional training, and having no contact with the conventional art world, naive artists likewise have not learned the conventional vocabulary of motives and explanations of their work. Since they cannot explain what they are doing in conventional art terminology, and since it can seldom be explained as anything other than art, naive artists frequently have trouble with people who demand an explanation. Not fitting into any conventional category, not legitimated by any authentic connection to an established art world, constructions like the Watts Towers, Clarence Schmitt's sculpture garden, Cheval's Palais Ideal, and the hundreds of similar works now being turned up by interested critics do require explanation (Cardinal, 1972). Since the makers provide none, they appear as the visible signs of eccentricity or madness. The maker easily becomes the object of ridicule, abuse, and even violence. Rodia was tormented by neighborhood kids and his Towers vandalized. Cheval (1968: 11), describing how he began to collect stones for the Palais, says: "Before long, local tongues began to wag . . . People actually thought I was mentally ill. Some laughed at me; some reproached or criticized me." When these artists do try to explain themselves and their work (and many do not), the explanations, having no conventional basis in some widely shared vocabulary of motive, may give substance to the suspicions of eccentricity. Here are some examples (Blasdell, 1968):

Mr. Tracy, of Wellington, Kansas, built a house out of bottles. His explanation of it was: "I saw a bottle house in California and they used only one kind of bottle, so I did them one better and used all kinds."

Herman Rousch, a farmer in Cochrane, Wisconsin, has made a work of art out of his house and grounds and explains what he has done thus: "Like it says, Mister, a mon should leave a few tracks and not just cancelled welfare checks."

S.P.D. Dinsmoor of Lucas, Kansas, says, "If the Garden of Eden (his name for the work of art he has constructed) is not right, Moses is to blame. He wrote it up and I built it."

Fred Smith said, "I'm 166 years old and I'll be better when I'm 175. It has to be in the man. You have to be almost gifted to do what I have done."

Just as the maverick quality of art lies in its relation to the conventional art world, so does the primitive quality of naive art. It is not the character of the work itself, but rather that it has been made without reference to the constraints of contemporary convention, that distinguishes naive art. This also makes understandable an otherwise knotty problem: does Grandma Moses' work remain naive once she has been discovered and the work exhibited in museums and galleries to critical acclaim? To the degree that she, or any "discovered" primitive, continues to ignore the constraints of the world into which she has now been incorporated, it remains what it was. To the degree that the artist begins to take account of what her new colleagues expect of her and are prepared to cooperate with, she has become an integrated professional, even though she has been integrated into a world which has somewhat changed itself to accommodate the variations she has created.

## Folk Art

In the final case I want to consider, that of folk art, no professional art community exists. Indeed, what is done is not really thought of as art at all, at least not by any of the people involved in its production, although people from outside the community or culture may find artistic merit in the work.

Within the community, most people, or most people of a particualr age and sex group, do that kind of work. They recognize that some do better at it than others, but that is a minor consideration; the main thing is that it be done to some minimum standard which is good enough for the purpose at hand. An excellent example in our culture is the singing of "Happy Birthday" at birthday parties. It matters very little if some of the singers are out of tune or tempo, as long as it gets sung; any competent participant in the culture can manage an acceptable version.

Folk artists (if we can speak of the community members who engage in these activities as artists at all) resemble canonical artists in being well integrated into a world in which the conventions of their art are well known and easily made the basis of collective action. No one finds it surprising that mountain women make patchwork quilts, and the kind they make and the standards by which they are judged are reasonably well expressed among all the members of their community. Peggy Goldie, an anthropologist who studied the aesthetic values of the inhabitants of Oaxaca, a village, tells of learning very quickly to distinguish which of the women potters in the village had made any particular pot, thinking by this means to demonstrate to these women that she understood the character of their artistic activity. Wishing to show off her skill, she one day remarked, "Oh, you made that pot, didn't you, Maria?" Maria first said she did not know whether she had made the pot and, on being prodded about it, said in effect that she could not understand why anybody would want to know a thing like that. In short, these women produced beautiful pottery, but were not oriented to our conventional notion that a person who makes a beautiful thing would be glad to be praised for it and would take the responsibility for having made it. The notion of a unique and artistic connection between artist and art work simply did not exist.

Because the artist constructs his art work with the help of other people who know just as much about it as he does, everyone being capable of playing any of the parts involved, cooperation comes about easily and with almost no friction, other than the ordinary friction of human intercourse. Bruce Jackson (1972) describes the way black convicts in Texas prisons coordinate their effort through the use of work songs, the songs providing the rhythm by which such activities as cutting down a tree can be safely carried out. Some men, he says, are better leaders of the singing than others, and everybody prefers it when they do the leading. Nevertheless, even a person who is not a good leader will serve the purpose as long as he can keep time. Anyone can lead, because everyone knows the song already. The leader's main function is simply to sing out the verses that they should use in singing the chorus. The leader takes the verses from a large pool of verses known to be parts of that song; everyone knows all the parts, and they need not be done in any particular order, nor need any particular number of combination of them be done on any particular occasion.

Of course, despite the similarity of all this to a conventional art world, in which everyone similarly knows his place and how to carry on the activity to be done, these folk communities are not artistic communities. They differ precisely in that the activity itself has some other purpose than an aesthetic one, and none of the people involved are "professional" artists. The good performers are not considered to be anyone special, but rather just ordinary community members who happen to be a little better at what is being done than the other members of the community.

## CONCLUSION

The four modes of being oriented to an art world—as integrated professional, maverick, grassroots artist, or folk artist—suggest a general scheme for interpreting the way people can be oriented to any kind of social world, no matter what its focus or its conventional round of collective activities. Insofar as the world has built up routine and conventional ways of carrying on those activities its members usually engage in, people can participate in it as fully competent members who know how to do easily and well whatever needs to be done. Most of what is done in that world will be done by people like that—the generalized analogue of integrated professionals. If the activity is one that every member of the society, or every member of some large subcategory engages in, the folk artist may provide a closer analogue. Some people, knowing what is conventional, will nevertheless choose to behave differently, with predictable ensuing difficulties in involvement in the world's collective activities. Some few of the innovations such people propose may be taken up by the larger world from which they have differed, making them into honored innovators (at least in retrospect) rather than cranks. Some will not know of the world's existence, or care much about it, and invent the whole thing for themselves—the generalized version of the naive artist.

In this way, we might say (with rather more warrant than it is usually said) that the world of art mirrors society at large.

## NOTES

1. Cage's music requiring performers to improvise their parts is heard, for example, in "Atlas Eclipticalis," Deutsche Grammophon 137009. One of Partsch's largest works is "Delusion of the Fury," Columbia M2 30576; this album includes a lecture by Partsch, explaining and demonstrating his instruments.

2. Nancarrow's "Studies for Player Piano" are available on Columbia MS 7222.

## REFERENCES

BECKER, H. S. (1974) "Art as collective action." Amer. Soc. Rev. 39(6): 767-776.
BIHALJI-MERIN, O. (1971) Masters of Naive Art. New York: McGraw-Hill.
BLASDELL, G. N. (1968) "The grass-roots artist." Art in America 56 (September-October): 25-41.
BLIZEK, W. L. (1974) "An institutional theory of art." British J. of Aesthetics 14 (September): 142-150.

CARDINAL, R. (1972) Outsider Art. New York: Praeger.

CHEVAL, F. (1968) "The fantastic palace of Ferdinand Cheval." Craft Horizons 28, 1: 8-15.

COWELL, H. and S. COWELL (1954) Charles Ives and his Music. New York: Oxford Univ. Press.

DANTO, A. (1964) "The artworld." J. of Philosophy, 61: 571-584.

DICKIE, G. (1971) Aesthetics: An Introduction. New York: Pegasus.

GOMBRICH, E. H. (1960) Art and Illusion: A study in the Psychology of Pictorial Representation. Princeton, N.J.: Princeton Univ. Press.

JACKSON, B. (1972) Wake Up Dead Man: Afro-American Worksongs from Texas Prisons. Cambridge: Harvard Univ. Press.

LEVINE, E. M. (1972) "Chicago's art world." Urban Life & Culture 1: 292-322.

LEWIS, D. K. (1969) Convention: A Philosophical Study. Cambridge: Harvard Univ. Press.

MEYER, L.B. (1956) Emotion and Meaning in Music. Chicago: University of Chicago Press.

MITCHELL, J. (1965) Joe Gould's Secret. New York: Viking.

PARTSCH, H. (1949) Genesis of a Music. Madison: Univ. of Wisconsin Press.

PERLIS, V. (1974) Charles Ives Remembered: An Oral History. New Haven, Conn.: Yale Univ. Press.

SMITH, B. H. (1968) Poetic Closure: A Study of How Poems End. Chicago: Univ. of Chicago Press.

TRILLIN, C. (1965) "I know I want to do something." New Yorker (May 29): 75-120.

WHITE, H. and C. WHITE (1965) Canvasses and Careers. New York: John Wiley.

*Using type of and control over rewards, Crane develops and illustrates the utility of a scheme for understanding variations among innovations in art, science, and religion.*

# Reward Systems in Art, Science, and Religion

DIANA CRANE
*University of Pennsylvania*

**In cultural institutions** such as the arts, the sciences, and religion where innovations are regularly produced, systems for evaluating innovations are necessary for the allocation of rewards. In order to understand the process of cultural innovation, it is necessary to examine how the social community in a particular cultural area rewards its members. Who sets the standards to which members of the community must conform? Who are the "gatekeepers" who evaluate the innovations produced by members of the community?

Based on a rationale developed earlier (Crane, 1972: ch. 8), I will argue that the elements of reward systems are the same in the arts, the sciences, and religion even though several types of reward systems can be identified in these three institutions which have different consequences for the production of innovations. It is not being suggested that innovations in science, the arts, and religion are similar in form, content, or intention—questions which have been discussed by some authors (see, for example, Meyer, 1974). Instead, I am proposing that the process of cultural innovation and change in all three

**Author's Note:** *The author is grateful to the Guggenheim Foundation for a fellowship which made possible the preparation of this paper.*

[57]

institutions can be described using the same model, whose parameters vary in different situations.

In the following pages, I will discuss examples from science, art, and religion which illustrate how alteration of various parameters of the model of a reward system affects the production of innovations and the nature of the innovations which are produced in these systems. The range of situations to which the model can be applied is enormous. My "data" will, of necessity, be derived from a review of existing studies, but I will also suggest new types of studies that need to be done.

## TYPES OF REWARD SYSTEMS

A major source of variation in the functioning of reward systems is the extent to which innovators control the system. Using this variable, one can develop a typology of reward systems which can be used to organize in a meaningful way the tremendous diversity of cultural innovations in modern society. Control over the reward system is indicated by who controls the key functions of the system—setting cognitive and technical norms and allocating symbolic and material rewards. Norms for the production of innovations are a central feature of reward systems. If an innovator wishes to win recognition for his innovations (Hagstrom, 1965; Gross, 1973), he must conform to the cognitive norms concerning the appropriate problems or themes for innovation. These may be embodied in either puzzle-solving devices or "world views" or both (Kuhn, 1970; Masterman, 1970). He must also follow technical norms concerning the appropriate methods and techniques for use in producing innovations.

Different types of standards are used for evaluating the extent to which an innovation has met the current cognitive and technical norms for such work. De Grazia (1963) has identified four sets of standards: (1) rational standards, which imply that an objective attempt is made to ascertain whether or not the innovative work has met the current cognitive and technical norms; (2) standards set by powerful gatekeepers who evaluate innovations in terms of whether or not "they preserve and enhance the power and prestige of the ruling group;" (3) dogmatic standards, which mean that new ideas are accepted to the extent that they conform to prevailing theories and norms; and (4) indeterminate standards, which mean that chance not quality affects the evaluation of an innovation and that the reception system for innovations is anarchic.

Reward systems in which innovators set cognitive and technical norms and allocate symbolic and material rewards can be contrasted with those in which they do some or none of these things. Innovations are produced, displayed, distributed, critiqued, and consumed in a wide range of social contexts, but four types of reward systems can be identified:

*(1) Independent reward systems* in which cultural innovations are produced for an audience of fellow innovators. Innovators themselves set cognitive and technical norms and allocate symbolic and material rewards. Examples of such reward systems are to be found in basic science and theology.

*(2) Semi-independent reward systems* in which innovators set norms for innovative work and allocate symbolic rewards, but material rewards are allocated by consumers, entrepreneurs, or bureaucrats. An example of this type of reward system is avant-garde art where innovators set norms, critics working very closely with innovators allocate symbolic rewards, and consumers allocate material rewards. In some areas of basic science, material rewards are increasingly being allocated by bureaucrats in government agencies.

*(3) Subcultural reward systems* in which cultural innovations are produced for an audience which represents a particular subculture. One type is an ethnic subculture, which is based on a variety of social characteristics that make it relatively permanent, enduring, and cohesive. A second type of subcultural reward system emerges because its members share a set of meanings, an interpretation of existence at a particular point in

time. These subcultures form to support the expression of certain types of attitudes, values, and social tensions and then disappear (Luckmann, 1967). A third type is the generational subculture. These subcultures usually appear among the younger members of society and disappear as the members age and become absorbed into other subcultures. Innovators set norms in subcultural reward systems, but consumers allocate symbolic and material rewards. Some examples of this type of reward system are black urban music (jazz), religious sects, and radical science.

*(4) Heterocultural reward systems* in which cultural innovations are produced for heterogeneous audiences composed of members of a variety of subcultures. This represents a situation in which entrepreneurs or bureaucrats set norms for innovative work, consumers allocate symbolic rewards, and entrepreneurs or bureaucrats allocate material rewards. Mass media artistic productions, so-called civil religion, and technology fall into this category. This type of cultural form is parasitic, borrowing from the other types if the gatekeepers think that these innovations will be of interest to a larger audience. New styles of innovation are frequently produced in the other types of reward systems and, if successful, are taken over by entrepreneurs in heterocultural systems.

The epitome of the heterocultural reward system involves innovations which are produced for the mass media. Hirsch (1972) has presented a detailed picture of this reward system, particularly as it operates in the most speculative and entrepreneurial segments of publishing, recording, and the motion picture industry. Typical of the heterocultural reward system is the supremacy of economic rewards over symbolic rewards and the fact that the innovator himself becomes relatively unimportant and powerless. He is easily replaceable by other innovators with whom he has little contact or exchange. Here the community of innovators is virtually nonexistent. Profit-making organizations control the resources for producing, displaying, and distributing innovations.

In this reward system, entrepreneurs in a set of profit-making organizations (film companies, publishing houses, and record companies) select innovations which they market to a mass audience of consumers. While there is a set of mass media critics who ostensibly play gatekeeping roles, they tend to be coopted by the entrepreneurs. Innovations are evaluated by the entrepreneurs in terms of the indeterminacy model: whether or not an innovation will be accepted is a matter of chance. The consumer's role is to rank-order preselected items. Hirsch says (1972: 649): "Feedback from consumers provides the clue as to which experiments should be imitated and which should be dropped."

In science, the analogous phenomenon is applied science and technology, where communities of innovators are generally confined within organizational boundaries and where cognitive and technical norms are set by management. Similarly, the elusive phenomenon known as civil religion does not include well-structured communities of innovators. Bellah (1967), for example, argues that there "exists alongside of and rather clearly differentiated from the churches an elaborate and well-institutionalized civil religion in America." It contains symbols of national solidarity and mobilizes deep levels of personal motivation for the attainment of national goals. Its appeal and support transcend the various subcultures of which the country is composed. It also seems likely that it is fostered by politicians in order to obtain a kind of pseudo-consensus in the country at large. Hammond (1968) suggests that one way this is done in the United States is through sports and other activities in the public education system.

By contrast, innovators in independent and semi-independent reward systems typically work in fairly cohesive communities. A number of studies of communities of innovators in science (Crane, 1972) have shown that these communities are centered around a few cohesive subgroups which are in communication with one another, but that there are always a certain number of isolates and many individuals whose commitment to the group is relatively transient. The subgroups have leaders who set standards for innovative work and recruit followers. Innovations are judged by innovators from neighboring areas who referee for scientific journals and granting agencies, award prizes, or hire staff members for academic departments. In other words, reward systems typically transcend communities of innovators. The latter compete for rewards with other communities that are producing innovations dealing with the same general subject matter. Similar studies of communities of innovators have not been done in avant-garde art or in theology, two other areas where innovations can be described as occurring in independent or semi-independent reward systems. However, there is some evidence from qualitative studies that analogous groups of innovators exist (White and White, 1965; Carey, 1973).

In independent reward systems, innovators control the resources for producing innovations (for example, academic departments and research institutes) and for displaying and distributing innovations (for example, scientific or scholarly journals). In semi-independent systems, innovators control either the resources for producing innovations or for displaying and distributing them, but not both.

In subcultural reward systems, the consumers play a much more important role. These communities probably consist of a small core of interacting innovators surrounded by a mass of consumers who share the innovators' key attitudes and values. The community is led by the innovators. The prototype is the religious sect or cult, but a number of folk traditions in music have analogous modes of organization. Examples can also be found in literature. Bradbury (1971: 181) has described literary periodicals which functioned as a medium of communication between writers and readers in the eighteenth and nineteenth centuries in England, maintaining a cultural dialogue between them:

> They select works, direct taste, review, judge, and influence both parties in literary communication. A good editor is a central cultural

mediator and the good magazine a stock of essential issues and a basic body of judgments.

In science, the subcultural reward system is rare, but cases can be found. Back (1971) has described how the group of researchers devoted to the study of the technique of sensitivity training gradually moved away from scientific evaluation of the technique toward the use of personal testimonials concerning the effectiveness of the method and at the same time attracted increasing numbers of adherents who were neither scientifically trained nor motivated. Similarly, radical science movements draw their membership from a wide variety of disciplines, including nonscientists, unlike other communities in basic science. In subcultural reward systems, innovators control the resources for producing innovations, but not for displaying or distributing them. However, the latter are not controlled by "big business," as in heterocultural reward systems.

To summarize, reward systems differ in terms of the cohesiveness of the relationships between innovators and in their control over the resources for producing, displaying, and distributing innovations. These factors, in turn, affect the amount of control which innovators are able to exert over the reward system.

## THE IMPACT OF REWARD SYSTEMS ON INNOVATION

Having described different types of reward systems, I will now discuss some factors affecting the nature of the innovations which are produced in them. Specifically, under what conditions can the innovations produced in these reward systems be characterized in terms of variety or continuity or both? "Variety" refers to the diversity of types or styles of innovations which are permitted within the same reward system as indicated by the number of different sets of cognitive and technical norms for innovations. "Continuity" refers to the extent to which subsequent innovations build on previous ones within the same set of cognitive and technical norms.

It can be argued that a high degree of continuity with little variety indicates that the range of acceptable types of innovations is being restricted by gatekeepers. If this is being done by innovators as gatekeepers, it probably reflects a shortage of rewards relative to the number of innovators in the system.

An example of the effect of relative scarcity of rewards upon the kinds of standards used to evaluate innovations is that of the French Academy in the nineteenth century (White and White, 1965; Mulkay and Turner, 1971). The French Academy operated a reward system for evaluating art objects and rewarding artists in which the gatekeeping functions were performed by members of the Academy; consumers played negligible roles. Success in the system depended upon receiving recognition from the Academy. In theory, the innovations were evaluated objectively; in practice, the gatekeepers increasingly attempted to maintain their own power and that of their followers. As the number of artists attempting to participate in the system increased, artists who were students of Academy members became more likely to win awards. Members of the Academy took turns over the years in obtaining symbolic rewards for their own students. There were often struggles between factions within the Academy, each presenting candidates for awards. In time, internal strains in the system led to the emergence of an alternative system for the allocation of artistic rewards.

Similar phenomena occur in science. Ben-David and Collins (1966; see also Ben-David, 1968) have stressed that the introduction of new disciplines in an academic system requires that the system be expanding in terms of the number of positions available. In other words, scarcity of resources in the system will make it more likely that those who already have positions will be less receptive to the introduction of new specialities or disciplines.

In other cases, the range of acceptable types of innovations will be restricted by gatekeepers who are not innovators. For example, entrepreneurs will do so in order to maintain their positions in a market. Peterson and Berger

(1975) describe how record companies limit the range of innovations in the popular music industry. They show that from 1948 to 1955 four large record companies controlled the popular music industry. This was possible because these firms controlled the media for merchandising music and channels for distributing records. Although the competition was intense, they had little incentive to innovate since they were aiming to capture the largest share of the total U.S. market. The popular music of the period was notable for its homogeneity: "it expressed a restricted range of sentiments in conventionalized ways."

In discussing theology, which is a source of cultural innovations within established churches, Schoof (1970) states that, before Vatican II, "the hierarchical teaching authority of the Catholic Church exerted an inhibiting and even paralysing influence on original thought of Catholic theologians." All attempts to innovate in theology were faced with criticism by the teaching authority which supported a particular kind of theology—neo-scholasticism—that was completely out of touch with the realities of the modern world and insensitive to changes that were taking place in secular society. The Church treated any questioning of this system as heresy. In terms of our model of reward systems, dogmatic rather than rational standards were being used to evaluate innovations. The gate-keeping role was performed by bureaucrats in an organizational hierarchy which reinforced their authority.

On the other hand, a high degree of variety (many different sets of cognitive and technical norms for innovation within the same reward system) with little continuity (little development within sets of cognitive and technical norms) represents an anomic situation where those who are allocating symbolic and material rewards do not consistently choose one style of innovation rather than another. Chance not quality affects the acceptance of innovations. There is some evidence that contemporary painting and sculpture represent an example of this kind of situation. Due to the high prices which can now be obtained for paintings, material rewards have become more

important than symbolic rewards. Consumers who allocate
material rewards tend to shift their choices from one style of
innovation to another. The increasing power of the consumer is
seen in the frantic production of innovations to attract his
attention (Kramer, 1974: 5). Many critics are displeased with
the situation. Kozloff (1967: 170) laments "the meaningless-
ness of the reward structure in contemporary art. In other
words, many, many establishments mean no establishment."
Analyzing a recent art movement, Kramer says (1973: 540):

> Under the guise of representing the latest 'advance' in avant-garde
> innovation, Pop art actually addressed itself to the largest possible
> audience—an audience that was suddenly and gratefully relieved of
> the necessity of having to deal with all the legendary difficulties that
> modernist art had always been said to interpose between the public
> and its ability to accept new artistic vocabularies. In place of
> complex ideas and hermetic images, of forms that had somehow to
> be parsed before they could be fully experienced, Pop offered a
> familiar iconography and a flip, easy irony. Everything in the new
> art was instantly recognizable, instantly assimilable . . . high culture
> was shown to be just another gag, another put-on, its despised
> scruples and distinctions an easily penetrated tissue of pre-
> tenses. . . . Pop art was never a mass art but it nonetheless enlarged
> the art public as nothing else ever had. . . . This new audience was
> not only without serious aesthetic experience . . . it was, in short, an
> audience thoroughly bemused by the myths of popular culture.

For both variety and continuity to be present in a reward
system, a number of conditions must be operating: (1) there
must be a balance between the availability of material resources
in relation to the number of innovators such that each
innovator has a reasonably good chance of being rewarded;
(2) symbolic rewards should be as important in the reward
system as material rewards. If the availability of material
rewards to the reward system declines, dogmatic or power
standards are likely to replace rational standards for the
evaluation of innovations, and this in turn leads to continuity
without variety. If symbolic rewards become less important
than material rewards, rational standards are likely to be

replaced by indeterminate standards, and this in turn leads to variety without continuity and a generally anomic situation in the entire system.

Reward systems in which either variety or continuity are stressed at the expense of the other are probably in an unstable state. Both situations are likely to lead to withdrawal from the system by innovators who feel that they are being discriminated against and the creation of a new reward system with new sets of cognitive and technical norms and a new set of gatekeepers, consumers, and display and distribution organizations. For example, some of the artists whose paintings were denied recognition by the French Academy eventually developed a new reward system.

## SHIFTS FROM ONE TYPE OF REWARD SYSTEM TO ANOTHER

One can also examine the conditions that lead a reward system to change from one type to another. For example, an independent reward system can become a heterocultural system or vice versa. Is there any indication that a particular type of reward system is beginning to predominate in modern societies? Two factors appear to be important here: (1) the relative control over resources for producing, displaying, and distributing innovations by innovators as compared to bureaucrats and entrepreneurs; and (2) changes in the possibilities for formation of social communities of innovators.

There is some indication that the dominant trend in modern societies is for independent, semi-independent, and subcultural systems to turn into heterocultural systems rather than vice versa. This reflects the increasing power of organizations that can take control of the resources for producing, distributing, or displaying innovations and interfere with the spontaneous formation of communities of innovators. This trend seems to be occurring in all three cultural institutions. Krohn (1972: 65-66) comments:

The dangers in a unique dependence on government support seem more obvious: how can science retain a critical measure of autonomy, self-discipline, and sense of direction? It is probably safe to say that no government has yet supported science on a modern scale and allowed it broad and intellectually autonomous development. The United States certainly does not seem to be immune to a narrow and direct use of science on government's terms.

Bradbury (1971: 194), describing the situation of the contemporary writer, states:

> The writer competes for attention with all the other happenings in our society. . . . The writer has lost a coherent literary community to appeal to, to test himself against, draw his sense of standards from . . . writing tends now to become part of the bland overall environment of the mass-culture situation itself. . . . Writers are uncertain about their values, their audience and their chances of survival.

At the same time, religious bureaucracies behave toward their "consumers" in some ways like the mass media oligopolists. Heirich (1974) describes the seven major religious groups in the United States (Roman Catholics, Baptists, Methodists, Lutherans, Jews, Presbyterians, and Episcopalians) as oligopolies which behave like large firms in consumer industries. They "dominate the field and engage in 'friendly competition' among themselves rather than follow the dictums of a strictly 'free market.' " As in the secular market, the result is a relatively homogenous religious product.

Certain kinds of cultural innovations are more susceptible to these trends than others, such as those where substantial resources are needed to produce, display, or distribute innovations or where profits are to be made from the sale of innovations in a market. Innovations which can be produced with minimal resources and which are not "commercial" are still being produced in the other types of reward systems. The case of black urban music (jazz) is an interesting counter-illustration of the trend. Thomson (1974) argues that this kind of music was saved from commercialization because audiences were concentrated in a few areas—mainly the slums of Chicago and Kansas City—and were easy to reach through live performances and by recordings put out by small companies. Thomson says:

> Its complete intolerance of anything but itself, its innate strength for rejecting impurities, made it virtually useless to big commerce. . . . Radical changes in both the style and expressive content of jazz have taken place with very little interference from outside.

Another counter-illustration of the trend is theology which is marginal to the religious "oligopolies" and thus "protected" from them (Berger, 1972). Catholic theology has become in the past decade the site of a profusion of movements and schools, advocating different types of interpretations of the contemporary religious situation. After Vatican II, the influence of the authoritarian, bureaucratic gatekeepers weakened, although it was not destroyed altogether. A shift away from a conception of theology as the formulation of dogma toward a conception of theology as a reflection on religion led to a period of considerable innovation. Carey (1973) identifies at least four types of movements within Catholic theology in the late 1960s, ranging from radical to conservative.

In some cases the trend has been reversed but probably only temporarily. Peterson and Berger (1971; 1975) discuss how, from time to time, the oligopoly of record companies in popular music is broken by independent producers and distributors who capitalize on the availability of markets of consumers who are not satisfied with the products of the record companies. The independents establish new cognitive and technical norms for popular music. These changes can be seen as shifts from heterocultural to subcultural reward systems which have resulted from loss of control over resources for distributing innovations by the major record companies.

The anomic conditions of contemporary art, where variety is stressed at the expense of continuity, have led to withdrawal from that system by some groups of innovators. For example, the artists who create what is called minimal art have chosen to break completely with the existing art establishment and to create paintings that are on the boundary between art and nonart (Battcock, 1968). This shift from a heterocultural back to a semi-independent reward system can perhaps be interpreted in part as the result of changes in the conditions affecting the formation of social communities of artists. As the number of dissidents increases, the possibility for the formation of groups of innovators expressing values counter to those of the establishment increases.

CONCLUSION

It has been suggested that four types of reward systems operate in the arts, the sciences, and religion. These reward systems vary in the amount of control which innovators exercise over the system in setting cognitive and technical norms for innovations and allocating symbolic and material rewards. Both groups of innovators and the reward systems to which they belong are constantly changing, developing, or transforming themselves in various ways which complicate the design of empirical studies.

This typology of reward systems suggests a number of areas for further research. What is needed are comparative studies, using the same conceptual framework, of cultural innovations that have previously been examined separately. Specifically, one might want to compare groups of innovators who are operating in the same type of reward system but located in different cultural institutions, or groups of innovators who are operating in different types of reward systems in the same cultural institution. It would also be useful to compare the effects of an external change upon different types of reward systems. For example, oligopolies are emerging in a number of cultural areas. How are they affecting the nature of innovations produced in these areas?

Finally, since we have argued that similar processes are occurring in each of the three cultural institutions, it would be of interest to examine the influence of one institution upon another. It seems plausible that the diffusion of ideas from one cultural institution to another would be most likely to occur via similar types of reward systems. This is because members of similar types of reward systems in different institutions probably share certain types of values, attitudes, and behaviors that lead to the formation of links from one social network to another.

# REFERENCES

ALBRECHT, M. C. (1973) "The arts in market systems." Presented at the annual meeting of the American Sociological Association, New York.

BACK, K. (1971) Beyond Words. New York: Russell Sage.

BATTCOCK, G. [ed.] (1968) Minimal Art: A Critical Anthology. New York: E. P. Dutton.

BELLAH, R. N. (1967) "Civil religion in America." Daedalus 96 (Winter): 1-21.

BEN-DAVID, J. (1968) Fundamental Research and the Universities. Paris: Organisation for Economic Development and Cooperation.

——— and COLLINS, R. (1966) "Social factors in the origin of a new discipline: the case of psychology." Amer. Soc. Rev. 31 (August): 451-465.

BERGER, P. (1972) "Religious establishment and theological education." Theology Today 19 (July): 178-191.

BRADBURY, M. (1971) The Social Context of Modern English Literature. New York: Schocken.

CAREY, J. P. (1973) "An overview of Catholic theology." Theology Today 30 (April): 25-41.

CRANE, D. (1972) Invisible Colleges: Diffusion of Knowledge in Scientific Communities. Chicago: Univ. of Chicago Press.

De GRAZIA, A. (1963) "The politics of science and Dr. Velikovsky." Amer. Behav. Scientist 7 (September): 33-37, 42-56.

GROSS, L. (1973) "Art as the communication of competence." Social Sci. Information, 12 (October): 115-141.

HAGSTROM, W. (1965) The Scientific Community. New York: Basic Books.

HAMMOND, P. E. (1968) "Further thoughts on civil religion in America," pp. 381-338 in D. R. Cutler (ed.) The Religious Situation: 1968. Boston: Beacon.

HEIRICH, M. (1974) "The sacred as a market economy." Presented at the annual meeting of the American Sociological Association, Montreal.

HIRSCH, P. M. (1972) "Processing fads and fashions: an organization-set analysis of cultural industry systems." Amer. J. of Sociology 77 (January): 639-659.

KOZLOFF, M. (1967) "Art criticism confidential," pp. 164-176 in J. E. Miller and P. D. Herring (eds.) The Arts and the Public. Chicago: Univ. of Chicago Press.

KRAMER, H. (1973) The Age of the Avant-Garde. New York: Farrar, Straus & Giroux.

KROHN, R. G. (1972) "Patterns of institutionalization of research," pp. 29-66 in S. Z. Nagi and R. G. Corwin (eds.) The Social Context of Research. New York: John Wiley.

KUHN, T. (1970) The Structure of Scientific Revolutions. Chicago: Univ. of Chicago Press, 2nd edition.

LUCKMANN, T. (1967) The Invisible Religion. New York: Macmillan.

MASTERMAN, M. (1970) "The nature of a paradigm," pp. 59-89 in I. Lakatos and A. E. Musgrave (eds.) Criticism and the Growth of Knowledge. Cambridge: Cambridge Univ. Press.

MERTON, R. K. (1973) "The normative structure of science," pp. 267-278 in R. K. Merton, The Sociology of Science. Chicago: Univ. of Chicago Press.

MEYER, L. B. (1974) "Concerning the sciences, the arts—and the humanities." Critical Inquiry 1 (September): 163-217.

MULKAY, M. J. and B. S. TURNER (1971) "Overproduction of personnel and innovation in three social settings." Sociology 5 (January): 47-61.

PETERSON, R. and D. G. BERGER (1975) "Cycles in symbol production: the case of popular music." Amer. Soc. Rev. 40, 2: 158-173.

——— (1971) "Entrepreneurship in organizations: evidence from the popular music industry." Admin. Sci. Q. 16 (March): 97-106.

SCHOOF, M. (1970) A Survey of Catholic Theology (N. D. Smith, trans.) Paramus, N.J.: Panelist Newman Press.

THOMSON, V. (1974) "Making black music." New York Rev. of Books 21 (October 17): 14-15.

WHITE, H. and C. WHITE (1965) Canvases and Careers. New York: John Wiley.

*DiMaggio and Hirsch describe the cycle from creation to consumption through which art is produced. Using an organizational model which could be applied to most culture-producing milieux, they focus on three levels of analysis: interpersonal, interorganizational, and total system.*

# Production Organizations in the Arts

PAUL DiMAGGIO
*Harvard University*

PAUL M. HIRSCH
*University of Chicago*

**Until recently** most sociologists have analyzed cultural products without attempting to understand how they were produced (cf. Sorokin, 1970); as Raymond Williams (1975: 5: 19) has put it, they have tended to "convert all processes into artifacts." Peterson (1976) has suggested that this practice tempts researchers into the normative realm of aesthetics; but as Max Weber (1949: 29) long since cautioned, the normal methods of sociology are of no help here because "an aesthetic evaluation

**Author' Note:** *Our names are listed alphabetically. We are indebted to Daniel Bell, Judith Lemon, Ann Orlov, Lauri Perman, Richard A. Peterson, Ann Swidler, and Harrison C. White for very valuable comments and criticisms on an earlier draft. The authors also gratefully acknowledge grants from the Rockefeller Foundation and National Science Foundation, to Paul Hirsch and Paul DiMaggio, respectively, which have made possible much of the research on which the article is based.*

cannot be arrived at with the means afforded by an empirical approach and it is indeed quite outside its province."

We follow the dictum of C. Wright Mills (1963: 406) to study the "cultural apparatus"—"all the organizations and milieux in which artistic, intellectual, and scientific work goes on, and . . . the means by which such work is made available to circles, publics and masses." Our research strategy is to examine and compare the diverse range of situations in which works of art are conceived, sketched, actualized, and enjoyed—processes which collectively will be termed the production of art. We adopt this perspective because as Hirsch (1972), Albrecht (1973), and Peterson (1976) have pointed out, it is naive to ask "How does society affect art?" or "What is the role of art in society?" or "What happens to art under socialism?" until we better understand the concrete range of activities and channels through which art is produced.

We will define "art" to include not only the so-called fine arts, but also popular culture, design, and the institutional networks which produce art and connect publics to producers—a realm which the aesthetician George Dickie (1974: 49) calls "the Byzantine complexity of the art world." Our topic thus encompasses a few things which everyone would consider art (painting, music, ballet, sculpture), and others which are aesthetic only secondarily (televised football games, commercial design, decisions by the Federal Communications Commission, and the like). There are good reasons for sociologists to use an organizational perspective and to define the arts so broadly. This strategy facilitates the search for communalities shared by several artistic media. It bypasses the debate neatly summarized by Lowenthal (1961) and Gans (1974) over the relative merits of high art and low. It also encompasses the general observation made by Becker (1974) that art media do not impose or constrain a particular division of labor in the production process. Numerous authors have shown that the division of labor in artistic production is based on consensual definitions of the situation which may change rapidly.[1]

Much of the conceptual apparatus to be employed here is drawn from industrial and organizational sociology and from the sociology of occupations and professions. It is used to facilitate our movement from the debate over what art *is*, to make possible comparisons across art forms, and to develop a scheme which may be useful for analyzing all culture-producing realms.

We shall discuss three organizational approaches to the study of artistic production systems. They range from micro to macro in focus. The first looks at functions, roles, and careers; the second emphasizes industries and processes; the third emphasizes total systems and complex interrelations among culture-producing institutions. These distinctions are heuristic and the perspectives are by no means mutually exclusive. In fact, most research studies utilize elements of the first two. In a sense, the perspectives are additive, for the first examines ways in which individual actors participate in the production of culture, while the second concentrates on the organizational arrangements by which these activities are integrated into a production system, and the third focuses on the ways in which this total cultural apparatus articulates with other societal institutions.

## FUNCTIONS, ROLES, AND CAREERS

This perspective takes the role occupant as its unit of analysis and emphasizes such factors as occupational socialization, norms and values, incentives, autonomy, role strain, and the social backgrounds of creators.[2] We will discuss four sets of essential functions—creation, entrepreneurship and patronage, promotion, and consumption—which must be performed to transform a work of art from a conception into a commodity.[3]

*Creation.* Creation in the arts can be individualistic. It can be sequential, as when one creator makes a plan or blueprint which can be executed by another with some degrees of freedom. It can be interactive, as in the negotiation between author and editor or between recording artist and producer. Or it can be corporate, as in the assembly of newspapers, motion pictures, network news, or "packaged texts."

Creation varies along several other dimensions as well. Some creators are employed by entrepreneurs; others work on a free-lance or independent basis. The skills of some are in great demand; others are subject to a buyers' market. Where training institutions are separate and to some extent insulated from the market, graduates may be ill equipped to face the demands of the artistic job market.[4] Ideologies differ as well: artists may conceive of themselves as creating for themselves, for critics, for elites, or for the "public." Attitudes towards critics, entrepreneurs, and the public differ accordingly (Truffaut, 1967). Artists in different settings use a variety of strategies to insulate themselves from the tension between their self-concepts as independent creators and their dependence upon external sources of financial support. One source of collegial support is the informal social circle (Coser, 1965; Gross, 1969; Znaniecki, 1940).

Of particular interest is the transformation of the creator's role in the face of organizational change. When artists in subcultural communities—each with its own system of values and stratification—begin to present their work to new and larger publics, some of their peers often respond with efforts to "keep the real faith," to enforce social control within the community. The fragility of artistic subcultures is indicated by their dependence on at least a minimum level of outside support; at the same time, they are vulnerable (and by the standards of most industries, distinctive) insofar as outsiders judge much of their output by criteria which they may not accept.

✳ *Entrepreneurship and patronage.* Art forms vary in the sources of support for their creation and dissemination. When someone other than the creator provides capital for the necessities of production, we speak of patronage (Henning, 1960; Collins, 1926; Haskell, 1963). When the capital is provided both for production *and* for distribution and promotion, we speak of entrepreneurship. The important questions here are: Who provides the capital needed for production and distribution? What do they want out of it? How do they attract the talent desired, and how do they screen the talent they do not want? How important is the need for innovative material compared to pressures for control of subordinates? Are selection decisions made by patrons or entrepreneurs themselves, under the guidance of professional consultants (Tomkins, 1973), by top managers of firms responsible to boards of directors or public authorities, or by middle managers under the gun of top management?

*Promotion and distribution.* Cultural products are disseminated in a variety of ways. An important distinction here is among systems where the means of distribution are owned by producers (e.g., movie theaters, when they were owned by large movie studios); are common carriers (e.g., the postal service); or are controlled by distributing agents, themselves gatekeepers who select a limited number of available items for sale or promotion (e.g., magazines on newsstands). Some gatekeepers are collectively absolute or nearly so—if all the galleries refuse to hang a painter's work, all the orchestras refuse to perform a composer's symphony, or all the television and radio stations refuse to broadcast a politician's speech, those products will reach the public with great difficulty, if at all. Other gatekeepers do not distribute, but are nonetheless important and sometimes vital for the publicity they provide. Two important examples in this society are radio stations (for the exposure they give phonograph records) and review media (especially for books and theater). A final kind of gatekeeping is performed by governmental gatekeepers (censors) or by pressure groups—district attorneys, religious organizations, feminist organizations, the FCC. Where gatekeepers present effective potential constraints, producers will utilize output-border specialists to cajole, mollify, and fix potentially threatening situations (Hirsch, 1969, 1972, 1975b).

*Consumption.* The size and nature of the audience are closely related to the organization of cultural production (Bourdieu, 1973; Maisel, 1973; Peterson and DiMaggio, 1975). Important variables here include the audience size associated with a particular art form; its social character (class, age, racial or ethnic make-up); and the social relations of consumption—individual or collective, passive or interactive. Again it is important to note that these factors are rarely inherent in technologies or art forms; usually they result from a certain kind of industrial organization or social structure. Economies of scale and sufficient publicity can result in a minority taste (such as country music) becoming a mass culture item. Restrictive funding and pricing policies, *avoidance* of publicity, and the engendering of a formal atmosphere at the point of consumption can maintain the eliteness of elite art (Arian, 1971), while different patterns of publicity, pricing, and framing may serve to break down barriers and stereotypes (Toffler, 1969; *Arts in Society,* 1975; Greyser, 1973). The social relations of consumption can also vary widely within a single medium. Video broadcasting, for instance, can deliver a program to millions of individual households, transmit a special event to a large crowd in a stadium, or enable two parties to communicate privately through a videophone. The significance of a medium or an art form to its audience may vary with the inclinations of those people who use it (Gans, 1974; Riesman, 1954), decisions made or fallen into for political or economic reasons (Williams, 1975), or the rise of new markets (Watt, 1957).

## THE INTERORGANIZATIONAL APPROACH

A second organizational perspective takes as its unit of analysis the industry or firm as a processing institution and concentrates on how industry structure and solutions to critical problems shape the final product. Such work often concentrates on market channels (Albrecht, 1973) or interorganizational or organization-environment relationships (Hirsch, 1975a, Thompson, 1967; Katz and Kahn, 1966; Burns and Stalker, 1961; Lawrence and Lorsch, 1967). By what stable organizational arrangements are the roles just outlined related and processed by a cultural system? Key issues amenable to study within this framework include innovation and control, control over substance, appraisal systems, internalization-externalization, unit size, and industry structure.

*Innovation versus control.* Cultural production systems are characterized by a constant and pervasive tension between innovation and control (Hirsch, 1972, 1975b; Peterson and Berger, 1975). Particularly in large market systems, but also in certain dealer-critic systems (Rosenberg, 1973; Wolfe, 1975), there is a substantial demand for new materials and new styles. At the same time, there are no clear formulas for novelty. Managers, creators, directors, and gatekeepers each develop their own criteria, all in an atmosphere of minimal direct feedback. Against the desire for novelty stands the desire for control; at the firm's input boundary, selectors and screeners attempt to make manageable an endless stream of proposals, manuscripts, demonstration tapes, resumes and portfolios that come their way.

The tension surrounding the input boundary leads to the odd, but usually rational, situation in which selectors expend immense amounts of energy seeking to ferret out the best talent (in terms of quality, potential sales, or, within limits, originality), while at the same time giving short shrift to the mass of would-be artists in search of sponsorship. In this setting, acquisition editors, talent scouts, agents, and others act formally as brokers, serving simultaneously to evaluate, select, and filter out new talent (Hirsch, 1972). Other input-border specialists, like "senior scholar-brokers" in scholarly publishing (Orlov, 1975), function less formally, by virtue of their position in social networks. This tension between innovation and control involves the simultaneous build-up and abandonment of stars (both creators and producers) and attempts to insulate the other operations of a firm from those involved in the creation of new cultural products (Peterson and Berger, 1971). There is some evidence that the promotion of cultural innovations is inhibited when sponsoring organizations can effectively block the entry of new competitors, face little competition, and/or fear political regulation (Peterson and Berger, 1975; Clark, 1973).

*Control over substance.* Closely related to the amount of innovation sought or permitted in a system is the substantive nature of the innovations allowed or forbidden. Typically, this type of control has been examined in the context of overt censorship (Sheavyn, 1909; Darnton, 1971). In western democracies, however, the locus of control has also been internalized within culture-producing systems, occurring with little direct intervention by government or pressure groups (Powdermaker, 1950; Peterson, 1967; Davis, 1975; Metz, 1975). This type of self-regulation is found partly because the size of the investment necessary in a market system to produce mass culture (and, to a lesser extent, fine arts) induces caution about the unknown; producers and distributors of popular culture, whose costs are highest, also tend to be the most sensitive to the threat of objections from organized pressure groups (Brown, 1971). In the United States, self-regulation has also tended to replace direct government intervention as public standards of obscenity, incitement to riot, and libel have become less stringent.

The etiology of conventions about what is and is not permissible (or, more broadly, "commercial") remains one of the sociology of art's outstanding mysteries, for culture-producing organizations do remarkably little research on the taste preferences of their publics. Most decisions appear to be based on what might best be called "imaginary feedback loops"— expectations about what a market, middleman, or federal or state agency *might* do if a certain line is crossed, a certain taboo violated (Gans, 1957; Bourdieu, 1971). Discovering the blueprints for imaginary feedback systems, and the ways in which they are formed and change, might provide the key to unlock the issue of information control in liberal societies.

*Appraisal: standards, homogeneity, and ambiguity.* There are different standards for gauging the success of different media or forms of art. The principal dimension for comparison is between market standards and critical standards (Bourdieu, 1971). Of course, there are different kinds of critical standards and different kinds of market standards. Even where standards are predominantly critical, critics will generally disagree, leaving standards ambiguous. Some critics have a structural base independent of the producers and distributors whose work they criticize. Others are tightly bound to the schools or art forms they criticize (Flippo, 1973-1974; Gruen, 1972; Wolfe, 1975).

Usually productions are dependent upon both critical and market determinants of success. Solutions to the tension between critical and box office standards have included the cooptation of creators with money and stardom; structural differentiation into high, middle, and low culture markets, each with different standards; and resignation to persistent acrimony and ambiguity.

*Internalization-externalization.* Industries vary in the extent to which different tasks are, on the one hand, centrally controlled and, on the other, contracted out to actors outside the entrepreneurial agency (Stinchcombe, 1959). Reasons for the decentralized, relatively professionalized organization of production in many cultural production systems include both minimization of overhead costs and uncertainty on the part of management as to what constitutes the right kind of innovation for critical or market success (Hirsch, 1972). In the United States, over the past thirty years, there appear to be two conflicting trends. On the one hand, vertical consolidation occurred when publishers bought printers and opened bookstores; magazines added staff writers and accepted fewer articles from free-lancers; and independent television producers encountered difficulties in gaining access to the medium. On the other hand, there has been much structural differentiation on the basis of function—for example, the rise of independent production in movies, recordings and, to a lesser degree, publishing. The extent of the structural integration of functions in the production of art appears to vary not only from field to field, but also within fields from year to year (Peterson and Berger, 1971, 1975).

*Market size and unit costs.* Two important dimensions here are size of market for new cultural products and the costs of their development and manufacture. Where markets are large and new product costs low, technical and substantive innovation will probably be fairly rapid and the products offered highly differentiated. Where markets are large and new product costs high, products will tend to be more marginally differentiated. Producers can expend great amounts of money on, for example, technical innovations, but they will be less willing to risk large losses on substantive innovation. Where markets are small and new product costs low, substantive innovation should be moderate or high but technical innovation low. Finally, where markets are small and new product costs high, industries may fail to develop.

*Industry structure: competition and market segregation.* Peterson and Berger (1975) have shown that the greater the number of competing firms in the popular music industry, the greater the diversity in types of music presented. A similar pattern seems to hold in the movie industry. Market segregation refers to the extent to which the products of an industry are specialized by function and market. Where segregation is greatest—for instance, between fine art painting and most magazine illustrations—there is little interaction between participants in the two systems, production never takes place under the same corporate roof, and distribution systems do not overlap. Somewhat less segregation exists between Hollywood and underground film: here there is at least some trading of personnel; however, ownership and distribution remain distinct. In book publishing, trade, paperback, and text may be divisions in the same corporation, and actors may interact professionally and informally; however, distribution systems are, for the most part, quite different. Finally, in the recording industry, rock, rhythm and blues, easy listening, and country music are all considered quite different genres; but they are all commissioned and manufactured by the same companies and often produced by the same producers; artists, writers, and songs "cross over" frequently; they are distributed to the same stores and, increasingly, played on the same radio stations. The extent of this type of market segregation may well affect both the rate and nature of innovation in a system and the amount of diversity available to consumers.

## THE TOTAL SYSTEMS APPROACH

A third organizational approach looks at the structure of the cultural apparatus itself—at relations among parts of industries that interact intensely and pervasively in ways which determine the nature of the art and communications media which are available throughout the world (Schiller, 1971; Altbach, 1975; Journal of Communication, 1974). The structure of these relationships—what Enzensberger (1974) refers to as "the consciousness industry"—often changes so quickly that no one, including participants, much less sociologists, has sufficient time to appraise the significance of the changes (Oettinger and Shapiro, 1975). The interrelatedness of different communications media and art forms has been noted in a host of historical and policy studies.[5] While the import of changes in the communications infrastructure for production in the arts, particularly the fine arts,[6] remains ambiguous, several themes are especially worth pursuing. It is important both to explore the significance of conglomerates for the production of culture, and to remain sensitive to enduring systems of informal complex organization discussed above.

The context of cultural production and distribution is, and has been, shifting continuously. Parts of the nineteenth-century American public, for example, encountered painting not in museums, which were not founded until the 1870s (Fox, 1963), but through lotteries and carnivals (Lynes, 1949: 19-20); hillbilly music reached some northeasterners via chautauguas, originally established to disseminate high culture (Peterson and DiMaggio, 1975). New media have often developed in response to changes in censorship policies, and their rise has in turn affected the operation of old media (Darnton, 1971). Currently, art forms and media continue to be swapped from industry to industry. The movie industry, for example, which has long purchased novels, is now beginning to favor original screenplays; and television, long a market for Hollywood movies, has lately been producing its own. As technological diversity allows the output of one artistic system to become the input for another, the complexity of institutional systems and the diffuseness of artistic boundaries increase. And as those systems become more integrated and the boundaries among them more diffuse, they also become less stable.

Another development of growing importance in the United States is the role of government policy in affecting the flow of cultural productions. For high culture this is a result of increased participation by the government in a number of spheres, particularly its involvement in high culture through the National Endowment for the Arts (Rockefeller Brothers Fund, 1965; Baumol and Bowen, 1968; Toffler, 1969). For popular media it is part of the tendency for federal arbitration, by regulatory agencies and courts, to become necessary as different technologies and corporate interests clash—e.g., cable and conventional television (*Yale Review of Law and Social Action,* 1972; Oettinger and Shapiro, 1975) or xerography and publishing (Breyer, 1970). As much of the world becomes one market both for high culture (Rosenberg, 1973: ch. 18) and for movies, recordings, and television programs, relations between governments and between multinational corporations and governments gain in importance. It therefore becomes essential that sociologists of art supplement their understanding of roles and norms with at least a rudimentary knowledge of political economy.

## CONCLUSIONS

In describing the sociology of art as a comparative study of organizations, we do not suggest that an organizational approach can provide answers to every interesting question about the arts. Rather we are setting forth a set of dimensions which should be useful in addressing a large number of researchable issues. Many of the major issues in the sociology of art can be rephrased profitably in organizational terms. Take, for instance, the question of whether art shapes society or society reflects art. Although most scholars have agreed that the process is dialectical, to really understand the relationship one needs to understand the social context of production—who produces art, what biases of selection make art which is produced and distributed systematically different from that which is not, and what political and economic factors influence the content of cultural products and the audiences to which they are directed.

The debate about whether art shapes or reflects society has often taken the form of the debate over culture under capitalism (or under socialism, depending upon the concerns of the period). Although they vary in the extent of their pessimism, Marcuse (1964), Enzensberger (1974), and Gramsci (1971) all argue that modern culture expresses different aspects of the "cultural hegemony" of the ruling class. Daniel Bell (1970), on the other hand, asserts that culture has become increasingly autonomous—that the cultural marketplace encourages the production and dissemination of material ultimately opposed to the values upon which capitalism is based, that "The breakup of the traditional bourgeois value system, in fact, was brought about by the bourgeois economic system—by the free market, to be precise." To evaluate either theory, it is useful to know, concretely, who creates culture, with whom in mind, and under what constraints.

Finally, there is the issue of the extent to which the structure of the distribution and consumption of culture reinforces the stratification system in any society. If, as Bourdieu (1973) suggests, individuals make their way through the world on the basis of "cultural capital" (and the "social capital" of friendships and alliances which accompanies it) as much as economic wealth, the extent to which prestigious cultural objects are restricted to intellectuals or elites will influence the stability of the class system. In other words, if the dominant culture is a code into which some people are inducted from birth and which others must master, debates over the value of cultural products and genres are, in many cases, highly political in nature. While these arguments are to some extent based on intangibles, looking at the socialization of producers of culture, the social contexts in which culture is produced, and the manner in which cultural items become joined and decoupled from particular social contexts may help shed light on the issues raised by Bourdieu.

These issues are all related to a central paradox of functional explanation: how can a system of actors with various motivations and individual agendas behave, in the aggregate, in a manner which appears rational (Gouldner, 1970)? That is, if Gramsci and Bourdieu are correct, by what processes does the quest of artists and their organizational associates for beauty, profit, truth, or fame come to act in support of an existing social structure? That paradox lies at the base of many of the core theoretical issues of the sociology of art and, as we have seen, at least part of its solution may be sought in the study of the organizations through which art is produced and disseminated.

## NOTES

1. See, for example, White and White (1965), Peterson (1967), Bourdieu (1971), Canter (1971), Noll et al. (1973), Barnouw (1975), Mosco (1975), and Metz (1975).

2. See Lane (1975), Becker (1957), Forsyth and Kolenda (1970), Burns (1972), Rosenberg and Fliegel (1965), Lester and Molotch (1974), Mueller (1951), and Cantor (1971).

3. These functions are similar to those set out by Hirsch (1969). They are set out here as functions rather than actors (e.g., creators, entrepreneurs) because of the numerous divisions of labor that have developed to handle them.

4. See Griff (1970), Strauss (1970), Faulkner (1973), Barron (1972), and Grana (1964).

5. Such studies include Pred (1973), Lynes (1949), Innis (1949), Bagdikian (1971), Deutsch (1966), Goldhamer and Westrum (1971), Barnouw (1975),

Hampton (1970), Goldberg (1930), Gillett (1970), Guback (1969), and Malone (1968).

6. The communications infrastructure and the structure of entertainment industries affect the "fine arts" in a number of ways. Not only do the fine arts draw ideas from the popular arts, but popular arts frequently provide substenance for individuals who make "fine art" in their spare time. What is more, the market for fine art is expanded and diversified by new technologies—for example, the impact of relatively high-quality poster production on the relative popularity of contemporary fine artists has yet to be assessed.

# REFERENCES

ALBRECHT, M. C. (1973) "The arts in market systems." Presented at the annual meeting of the American Sociological Association, New York.
——— (1968) "Art as an institution." Amer. Soc. Rev. 33: 383-397.
ALTBACH, P. G. (1975) "Literary colonialism: books in the third world." Harvard Educ. Rev. 45: 226-36.
ARIAN, E. (1971) Bach, Beethoven and Bureaucracy: The Case of the Philadelphia Orchestra. University, Ala.: Univ. of Alabama Press.
Arts in Society (1975) Special issue: "The surge of community arts."
BAGDIKIAN, B. (1971) The Information Machines: Their Impact on Men and Media. New York: Harper & Row.
BARNOUW, E. (1975) Tube of Plenty: The Evolution of American Television. New York: Oxford Univ. Press.
BARRON, F. et al. (1972) Artists in the Making. New York: Seminar.
BAUMOL, W. J. and W. G. BOWEN (1968) Performing Arts: The Economic Dilemma. Cambridge: MIT Press.
BECKER, H. S. (1974) "Art as collective action." Amer. Soc. Rev. 39: 767-76.
——— (1957) "The professional dance band musician and his audience." Amer. J. of Sociology 57: 136-44.
BELL, D. (1970) "The cultural contradictions of capitalism." Public Interest, no. 21: 16-43.
BOURDIEU, P. (1973) "Cultural reproduction and social reproduction," in R. Brown (ed.) Knowledge, Education and Cultural Change. London: Tavistock.
——— (1971) "Intellectual field and creative project," in M.K.D. Young (ed.) Knowledge and Control. London: Macmillan.
BREYER, S. (1970) "The uneasy case for copyright: a study of copyright in books, photocopies, and computer programs." Harvard Law Rev. 84: 281-351.
BROWN, L. (1971) Television: The Business Behind the Box. New York: Harcourt-Brace-Jovanovich.
BURNS, T. (1972) "Commitment and career in the BBC," in D. McQuail (ed.) Sociology of Mass Communications. Middlesex: Penguin.
——— and G. M. STALKER (1961) The Management of Innovation. London: Tavistock.

CANTOR, M. C. (1971) The Hollywood TV Producer. New York: Basic Books.

CLARK, T. (1973) Prophets and Patrons: The French University and the Emergence of the Social Sciences. Cambridge: Harvard Univ. Press.

COLLINS, A. S. (1926) "Patronage in the days of Johnson." Nineteenth Century 100: 608-22.

COSER, L. A. (1965) Men of Ideas. New York: Free Press.

DARNTON, R. (1971) "Reading, writing and publishing in eighteenth-century France: a case study in the sociology of literature." Daedalus 10.

DAVIS, C. (1975) Clive: Inside the Record Business. New York: William Morrow.

DEUTSCH, K. (1966) The Nerves of Government: Models of Political Communication and Control. New York: Free Press.

DICKIE, G. (1974) Art and the Aesthetic: An Institutional Analysis. Ithaca, N.Y.: Cornell Univ. Press.

ENZENSBERGER, H. (1974) The Industrialization of the Mind. New York: Seabury.

FAULKNER, R. (1973) "Career concerns and mobility motivation of orchestra musicians." Soc. Q. 14.

FLIPPO, C. (1973-1974) "The history of *Rolling Stone*." Popular Music & Society 3: 159-88, 258-98.

FORSYTH, S. and P. KOLENDA (1970) "Competition, cooperation, and group cohesion in the ballet company," in M. C. Albrecht, J. H. Barnett, and M. Griff (eds.) The Sociology of Art and Literature. New York: Praeger.

FOX, D. M. (1963) "Engines of culture: philanthropy and art museums."

GANS, H. J. (1974) Popular Culture and High Culture. New York: Basic Books.

––– (1957) "The creator-audience relationship in the mass media: an analysis of movie making," in B. Rosenberg and D. M. White (eds.) Mass Culture: The Popular Arts in America. New York: Free Press.

GILLETT, C. (1970) The Sound of the City. New York: Outerbridge & Dienstfrey.

GOLDBERG, I. (1930) Tin Pan Alley. New York: Frederic Ungar.

GOLDHAMER, R. and R. WESTRUM (1971) The Social Effects of Communications Technology. Santa Monica: Rand Corporation.

GOULDNER, A. (1970) The Coming Crisis of Western Sociology. New York: Basic Books.

GRAMSCI, A. (1971) The Prison Notebooks. New York: Harper & Row.

GRANA, C. (1964) Bohemian Versus Bourgeois. New York: Basic Books.

GREYSER, S. A. [ed.] (1973) Cultural Policy and Arts Administration. Cambridge: Harvard Summer School Institute in Arts Administration.

GRIFF, M. (1970) "The recruitment and socialization of artists," in M. C. Albrecht, J. H. Barnett, and M. Griff (eds.) The Sociology of Art and Literature. New York: Praeger.

GROSS, J. (1969) The Rise and Fall of the Man of Letters. New York: Collier.

GRUEN, J. (1972) The Party's Over Now. New York: Viking.

GUBACK, T. H. (1969) The International Film Industry: Western Europe and America Since 1945. Bloomington: Indiana Univ. Press.

HAMPTON, B. (1970) History of the American Film Insustry from Its Beginnings to 1931. New York: Dover.

HASKELL, F. (1963) Patrons and Painters: A Study in the Relations Between Italian Art and Society in the Age of the Baroque. New York: Alfred A. Knopf.

HENNING, E. (1960) "Patronage and style in the arts: a suggestion concerning their relations." J. of Aesthetics & Art Criticism 18: 464-471.

HIRSCH, P. M. (1975a)"Organizational analysis and industrial sociology: an instance of cultural lag." Amer. Sociologist 10: 1-12.

——— (1975b) "Organizational effectiveness and the institutional environment." Admin. Sci. Q. 20: 327-344.

——— (1972) "Processing fads and fashions: an organization-set analysis of cultural industry systems." Amer. J. of Sociology 77: 639-659.

——— (1969) The Structure of the Popular Music Industry. Ann Arbor: University of Michigan, Institute for Social Research.

INNIS, H. (1949) Empire and Communication. Oxford: Clarendon.

Journal of Communication (1974) "Cultural exchange or invasion?–a symposium." Vol. 24: 89-117.

KATZ, D. and R. L. KAHN (1966) The Social Psychology of Organizations. New York: John Wiley.

LANE, M. (1975) "Shapers of culture: the editor in book publishing," in P. C. Altbach and S. McVey (eds.) Perspective on Publishing. Annals of the Amer. Academy of Pol. & Social Sci. 421.

LAWRENCE, P. and J. LORSCH (1967) Organization and Environment. Cambridge: Harvard University, Graduate School of Business Administration.

LESTER, M. and H. MOLOTCH (1974) "News as purposive behavior." Amer. Soc. Rev. 39: 101-112.

LOWENTHAL, L. (1961) Literature, Popular Culture, and Society. Englewood Cliffs, N.J.: Prentice-Hall.

LYNES, R. (1949) The Tastemakers. New York: Harper.

MAISEL, R. (1973) "The decline of the mass media." Public Opinion Q. 37: 159-171.

MALONE, B. C. (1968) The Country Music Story. Austin: Univ. of Texas Press.

MARCUSE, H. (1964) One Dimensional Man. Boston: Beacon.

METZ, R. (1975) CBS: Reflections in a Bloodshot Eye. New York: Playboy Press.

MILLS, C. W. (1963) "The cultural apparatus," in I. L. Horwitz (ed.) Power, Politics and People. New York: Oxford Univ. Press.

MOSCO, V. (1975) The Regulation of Innovation in the Broadcasting Market. Cambridge, Mass.: Program on Information Technologies and Public Policy.

MUELLER, J. H. (1951) The American Symphony Orchestra. Bloomington: Indiana Univ. Press.

NOLL, R. G., M. J. PECK, and J. J. McGOWAN (1973) Economic Aspects of Television Regulation. Washington, D.C.: Brookings.

OETTINGER, A. G. and P. D. SHAPIRO (1975) Information Industries in the United States. Cambridge, Mass.: Program on Information Technologies and Public Policy.

ORLOV, A. (1975) "Demythologizing scholarly publishing," in P. G. Altbach and S. McVey (eds.) Perspectives on Publishing. Annals of the Amer. Academy of Pol. & Social Sci. 421.

PETERSON, R. A. (1976) "The production of culture: a prolegomenon." Amer. Behav. Scientist 19 (July-August): 669-684.

——— (1967) "Market and moralist censors of a rising art form: jazz." 4: 253-264.

——— and D. G. BERGER (1975) "Cycles in symbol production: the case of popular music." Amer. Soc. Rev. 40: 158-173.

——— (1971) "Entrepreneurship in organizations: evidence from the popular music industry." Admin. Sci. Q. 16: 97-106.

PETERSON, R. A. and P. DiMAGGIO (1975) "From region to class, the changing locus of country music: a test of the massification hypothesis." Social Forces 53: 497-506.

POWDERMAKER, H. (1950) Hollywood: The Dream Factory. New York: Grossett & Dunlap.

PRED, A. R. (1973) Urban Growth and the Circulation of Information: The United States System of Cities, 1790-1840. Cambridge: Harvard Univ. Press.

RIESMAN, D. (1954) "Listening to popular music," in Individualism Reconsidered. New York: Free Press.

Rockefeller Brothers Fund (1965) The Performing Arts: Problems and Prospects. New York: McGraw-Hill.

ROSENBERG, B. and M. FLIEGAL (1965) The Vanguard Artist: Portrait and Self-Portrait. Chicago: Quadrangle.

ROSENBERG, H. (1973) The Anxious Object: Art Today and Its Audience. New York: Collier.

SCHILLER, H. J. (1971) Mass Communications and American Empire. Boston: Beacon.

SHEAVYN, P. (1909) The Literary Profession in the Elizabethan Age. Manchester: Manchester Univ. Press.

SOROKIN, P. (1970) Social and Cultural Dynamics. Boston: Porter Sargent.

STINCHCOMBE, A. (1959) "Bureaucratic and craft administration of production." Admin. Sci. Q. 4: 168-187.

STRAUSS, A. (1970) "The art school and its students: a study and an interpretation," in M. C. Albrecht, J. H. Barnett, and M. Griff (eds.) The Sociology of Art and Literature. New York: Praeger.

THOMPSON, J. D. (1967) Organizations in Action. New York: McGraw-Hill.

TOFFLER, A. (1969) The Culture Consumers. New York: St. Martin's.

TOMKINS, C. (1973) Merchants and Masterpieces. New York: E. P. Dutton.

TRUFFAUT, F. (1967) "Le savate et la finance, ou deux ou trois choses que je sais de lui." L'Avant-Scene du Cinema no. 70.

WATT, I. (1957) The Rise of the Novel. London: Chatto & Windus.

WEBER, M. (1949) "The meaning of ethical neutrality," in E. A. Shils and H. A. Finch (eds. and trans.) The Methodology of the Social Sciences. New York: Free Press.

WHITE, H. C. and C. A. WHITE (1965) Canvasses and Careers: Institutional Change in the French Painting World. New York: John Wiley.

WILLIAMS, R. (1975) Television: Technology and Cultural Form. New York: Schocken.

WOLFE, T. (1975) "The painted word." Harper's (April): 57-92.

Yale Review of Law and Social Action (1972) Special issue: "The cable fable." No. 3 (Spring).

ZNANIECKI, F. (1940) The Social Role of the Man of Knowledge. New York: Columbia Univ. Press.

*Hagstrom employs a production perspective to integrate what is known and reveal what is not known about the relationship between the subject matter of scientific specialties and the structure of the research groups. He also compares the structure of science and engineering work groups.*

# The Production of Culture in Science

WARREN O. HAGSTROM
*University of Wisconsin*

**Metaphor** has always played an indispensable role in the development of scientific theories as well as in the development of other types of culture (Kaplan, 1964: 258-288). The notion of the production of culture is such a metaphor, suggesting how we can apply theories about the production of commodities and services to culture and perceive similarities among diverse realms of culture. I shall proceed by taking the metaphor seriously, and I will only briefly indicate some of the problems that may be produced by taking it too seriously. However, I cannot forbear pointing out that this notion that culture may be produced like anything else has long since been savagely criticized. Almost 250 years ago Jonathan Swift satirized the notion in *Gulliver's Travels.* He describes the Grand Academy of Lagado, one of the projects of which was "for improving speculative knowledge, by practical and mechanical operations," in which "the most ignorant person, at a reasonable charge, and with a little bodily labour, might write books in philosophy, poetry, politics, laws, mathematics, and theology, without the least assistance from genius or study" *(Gulliver's Travels,* Part III, ch. V, first published 1726). How might Swift react to the fact that there is now a small industry producing culture about him! In the 40 years prior to 1967, about 600 books and articles about him and his work appeared (Mayhew, 1967: 187), and in 1973 alone, 33 works on Swift were published by as many authors *(Philological Quarterly,* 1974).

Anyway, scientists work on nature, applying human, animal, and inanimate energy to produce information which, suitably processed, is disseminated to consumers. I shall begin by discussing the organization of work groups in science, proceed to discuss the coordination of the activities of related groups, continue to consider the dissemination of products to ultimate consumers, and conclude by considering some of the limitations of the metaphor as it pertains to the consumption, destruction, or transformation of scientific culture. I will not trouble much to make explicit comparisons with other realms of culture, though potential similarities and differences should be apparent throughout.

## THE ORGANIZATION OF WORK GROUPS

Scientific research implies ignorance and uncertainty. The uncertainty is primarily in the task or technology domain; the uncertainty about the provision of resources or the marketing of products is much less serious. The degree of uncertainty varies considerably among the sciences. When the production of information about the empirical world is most highly routinized, workers are likely to be characterized not as scientists, but as technicians.

Charles Perrow (1967, 1972), March and Simon (1958: 141 ff.), and others have pointed out how varying degrees of uncertainty affect several characteristics of organizations. Uncertainty is reduced and behavior capable of being routinized when workers deal with uniform types of problems and when the search for ways to deal with exceptions is seldom needed or easily accomplished. These theories have been applied to science by Lowell Hargens (1975: ch. III) in a comaprative study of mathematicians, chemists, and political scientists. He found the work of mathematicians least routinized (cf. Fisher, 1973).

Mathematicians will say such things as "I feel that I'm stuck most of the time. The real question seems to be whether or not there is any period when I'm not stuck," and "Sometimes I spend literally weeks to find a two-line proof. Usually, I'm just waiting around for something to happen" (Hargens, 1975: 40 ff.). By contrast, work in political science and chemistry is more routine, chemistry being the most routinized of the three fields on most indicators. Hargens found that the more routinized the field, the better able workers were to get things done by planning work in detail and by setting deadlines for themselves. Correspondingly, in the more routinized fields, a larger amount of the variance in research productivity could be explained by the amount of time spent on research and the scientists' subjective evaluations of their own personal efficiency.

When work is relatively routine, scientists are enabled to delegate many tasks to less-skilled subordinates, usually graduate students, but also technicians and postdoctoral fellows. Chemists especially, but political scientists too, have more assistance than mathematicians, and the amount of assistance can account for well over half the variance in the productivity of chemists, much less but still a significant amount of the variance in productivity of political scientists, and essentially none of the variance in productivity of mathematicians. Chemists, then, rationally attribute low productivity to a lack of assistance. Mathematicians are more likely to attribute their low productivity to their personal deficiencies, and thus mathematicians are more likely to be depressed by periods of low productivity than those in the other two fields.

As Randall Collins has noted (1975: 506-514), Joan Woodward's (1965) theory of the relation between technology and the structure of organizations can be applied readily to science. Given the typically nonroutine nature of scientific work, it can be characterized as prototype, unit, or small batch production. Following Woodward, we would expect work groups to be relatively small, work to be relatively labor-intensive, and a high proportion of workers engaged in direct production instead of support services. Work groups should have few hierarchical levels, there should be a low span of control, and there should be a high ratio of supervisory personnel to those supervised. Most science is little science, and the data we have about work groups are consistent with the preceding hypotheses. In my survey of representative samples of academic scientists (Hagstrom, 1967, 1974), I found that work groups averaged in size from about four in mathematics to more than nine in experimental physics. While most scientists in all the fields I surveyed reported collaborating with persons of faculty rank, graduate students were the most important components in every field. The importance of young persons employed at substandard wages is common in almost all types of culture.

Consistent with the preceding discussion, I found that work groups are smallest in the least routine field, mathematics. Other differences among fields are also affected by technology. Chemistry epitomizes a labor-intensive field. Professors of chemistry can work quite autonomously with workers and apparatus under their exclusive control. The relative independence of work groups in chemistry permits a lower degree of collaboration among faculty peers: 44% of the chemists reported collaborating with peers, in contrast to 68% of the experimental physicists, and 61% of the biologists. When such collaboration exists in chemistry, it is likely to be informal and to involve a clear division of labor—chemists collaborate when they are compelled to do so because they lack the needed skills.

As in almost any labor-intensive area of work, attempts are made to mechanize and automate work by substituting capital for labor. In chemistry this has tended to occur without producing major changes in the organization of work groups. Thus, most of the chemists in my survey were using analytic instruments invented in the preceding 15 years and sometimes based on discoveries made in that inverval; but the apparatus is such that it usually can be operated by the chemist himself and his small number of relatively untrained assistants.

In other areas of science, the nature of research problems as well as a desire to substitute capital for labor have led to those major changes in the nature of work we call big science. There is no clear-cut demarcation between little science and big science, and not all big science is capital-intensive. Big science is epitomized by high energy physics. Despite labor-saving devices, the work groups at high energy particle laboratories can be very large. For example, in 1964 the research staff at the Lawrence Radiation Laboratory in Berkeley was divided into about 11 groups; outside groups also used the Laboratory's accelerators. The smallest group had 12 professional personnel. The largest included 160 full-time-equivalent personnel—23 Ph.D.s, 20 graduate students, and numerous others, including cryogenic engineers, mathematical programmers, computer technicians, and still others for more routine tasks (Swatez, 1970). As one might expect, such large batch production in science involves a greater division of labor—but primarily among subordinate personel, not the professional physicists who lead the groups. There is a much higher proportion of highly trained auxiliary personnel, a broader span of control, and greater centralization of decision-making. However, the "centralization" of work groups in such large batch production tends to be like that of innovative firms in industries with uncertain environments (cf. Ritti and Goldner, 1969: B-240 ff.). The top decision-makers do not so much initiate actions for subordinate scientists as make choices among alternative courses of actions suggested by subordinates. Subordinate Ph.D. scientists, and even graduate students, suggest experiments and are expected to do so.

In most cases big science has not meant an abandonment of small batch production in science. Scarce and expensive research facilities, such as computer centers or survey research laboratories, often can be organized in such a way as to provide small work groups with routinized services on demand.

## THE COORDINATION OF ACTIVITIES AMONG WORK GROUPS

The work groups I have been discussing are ordinarily embedded in larger organizations. Universities and governmental or industrial establishments can be seen as providing support services and as sanctioning or specifying goals; I will be unable to give such organizations the attention they deserve here. In addition to such formal organizations, each work group is likely to be linked to other groups working on the same or related research problems. Such links are likely to be informal, and the groups are usually found in different formal organizations. The plural number of groups working in a problem area probably stems mostly from the nature of the tasks confronting them: no one group is likely to be perceived capable of solving all those problems felt to require solutions. It is also motivational: linked groups provided the most important audiences for the work of each.

These sets of groups are difficult to label or conceptualize. Considering their structure, one is led to call them networks or, more precisely, clusters in networks. Considering the intellectual content of their work, or their positions in encompassing disciplinary organizations, one is led to call them specialties or subspecialties. Considering the history of such groups, the most felicitous label might be "invisible colleges" (Price, 1963: ch. 3). Different network clusters vary considerably in size, interconnectedness, internal stratification, clarity of boundaries, and visibility to members and non-members. Yet they are ubiquitous and, perhaps, the most important level of the social organization of science.

These network clusters can be viewed as production organizations. From the point of view of an organizational administrator, they might seem to be hopelessly irrational "organizations." There is seldom any effective control over network membership; groups may enter or leave easily. There is almost never coordinated planning or control; no agencies exist to direct component groups to work on particular problems. As a result, there is considerable duplication of effort, and most scientists are concerned that others may publish solutions to their problems before they can succeed in doing so (Hagstrom, 1974). Yet, given the uncertainty of the task environment and the relative beneficence of the support and market environments, this loose form of organization may lead to more effective coordination of the efforts of different groups than any alternative form. Given task uncertainty, effective coordination cannot be achieved through planning or centralized direction. The alternative is more or less rapid feedback through formal and informal communication among the component groups in network clusters. This type of coordination requires that scientists spend a far larger fraction of their time in communicative behavior than most other types of workers.

It is difficult to estimate the typical size of clusters in these networks, since groups often enter or leave, and some groups are only loosely attached. It is safe to say that they are typically small. Derek Price's 1963 guess that the *maximum* size of an invisible college is 100 cannot be far wrong. On the basis of numerous case studies, I would estimate that the average number of individual professional workers closely linked together in networks is less than 50; the effective network component is ordinarily a work group, and thus the average number of closely linked groups in networks must be less than 50. (For case studies and estimates, see Hagstrom, 1967 and 1974; Crane, 1972; and Griffith and Miller, 1970.) The autonomy of work groups, and the linking together by loose ties of work groups throughout a discipline (cf. Granovetter, 1973), make it possible for the effective size of network clusters to expand rapidly, a growth potential demonstrated by numerous studies, in particular Diana Crane's *Invisible Colleges* (1972).

Members of scientific networks share with one another those related commitments Thomas Kuhn has called "paradigms"—or, in words more true to Kuhn, the network cluster *is* one aspect of that "disciplinary matrix" constituting a paradigm (Kuhn, 1970). Members share commitments to values, metaphysical paradigms, heuristic models, and examplars. Thus, they can communicate with one another without first having to negotiate a consensus about fundamental values and meanings, and they can coordinate their activity to solve scientific problems because of shared convictions that the problems are paradigm-induced "puzzles" with assured solutions.

In the language of the organization theory of March and Simon (1958), one can view the network cluster as an organization that both constrains and facilitates the work of its members. While such network clusters are very much different form the well-bounded and hierarchical firms about which Simon and his colleagues wrote, it is clear that they operate to socialize individual members, to reward conformity, and to punish deviance. Just as paradigms function to enable scientists to solve puzzles in the absence of explicit rules and the presence of anomalous data, so the organization, for March and Simon, facilitates local rationality and "satisficing" behavior in situations where optimizing behavior is impossible. The organization does this by specifying goals, fostering *limited* search processes that are only mildly innovative, focusing attention on a restricted range of stimuli, providing programs and repertoires of action that do not require a process of optimal decision-making at every turn, and in other ways not so relevant to science. There is, thus, a close similarity in the opposition between the March-Simon model of organizational rationality and classical optimizing models, on the one hand, and the opposition between Kuhn's notion of normal science and Karl Popper's ideal of permanently revolutionary science (see Lakatos and Musgrave, 1970), on the other. That is, debates about rationality in science are like debates about rationality in organizations—perhaps because of fundamental similarities in the nature of human rationality.

Kuhnian normal science is inadequate to characterize the organization of science in at least two situations. The first is that of crisis and revolution, which he discussed in detail. When a paradigm cannot successfully resolve critical anomalies, a revolutionary situation may arise. At such times fundamental values and beliefs can no longer be taken for granted, and at such times communication may break down. As Kuhn puts it, in revolutionary situations those committed to competing paradigms may seem to speak in different languages. It is possible that productivity may decline in such critical periods, although in the one case I know of, such a situation coincided with increased productivity in the parity nonconservation crisis of weak interaction physics around 1956 (Sullivan et al., 1975).

A second situation deviating from normal science may occur when a preponderance of scientists are not linked to others in network clusters. This may be a common characteristic of preparadigmatic and multiparadigmatic fields, and it may result from pathological overspecialization as in mathematics. Following Durkheim, I have earlier suggested that such situations can be characterized as anomic and will have the characteristics expected of anomic societies (Hagstrom, 1964, 1965; see also Hargens, 1975). Workers have little social confirmation of the value of their own products and thus vacillate from attributing absolute value to them—"mathematics for mathematics' sake"—to having pervasive doubts about their value and, since scientists identify themselves with their work (cf. Stinchcombe, 1966), pervasive doubts about their own self-worth. They may become ritualistic, continuing to produce when they have no confidence that their work will be appreciated or used by others. It is reasonable to believe that productivity will decline in such anomic situations.

While anomie is probably less common in science than in art and music, those sociologists of art and music among my readers probably know from first-hand experience what it is like to work in an anomic field. Anomie implies a lack of paradigms in the Kuhnian sense: one does not find, simultaneously, an integrated group, shared values, models, and exemplary works. Each worker in the sociology of art has tended, in Kuhn's words, to create the field anew. Few have found it possible to select, as research problems, puzzles existing in prior exemplars, nor can they confidently use the methods of the exemplars to solve their puzzles. Each worker has had to try to create anew his own "invisible college," and many have been tempted to optimize by solving "fundamental" problems rather than "satisfice" by working on smaller soluble problems. It is not easy. (On the other hand, work in nonparadigmatic fields is not necessarily inferior, as evidenced by the work of such scientists as Louis Pasteur, Gregor Mendel, and Sigmund Freud in such fields.)

## DISTRIBUTION AND CONSUMPTION

Before the professionalization and institutionalization of science in the nineteenth century, scientists often disseminated their discoveries directly to an elite clientele in settings that required entertainment as well as edification. Michael Faraday lectured gentlemen and ladies at the Royal Institution of London, and he wrote that polite audiences "expect to be entertained not only by the subject of the lecture, but by the manner of the lecturer; they look for respect, for language consonant to their dignity, and ideas on a level with their own." (Crowther, 1935: 81). Similar statements could have been made by Robert Hooke about his work for the Royal Society around 1700, when he was expected to prepare an interesting experiment about every other week, and by the workers in similar institutions in Europe in the eighteenth century. Hooke, Faraday, and others managed to be quite productive in such settings, in part because they were linked into the kind of informal networks of scientists that have been described above.

In modern science products are disseminated through channels controlled almost completely by the scientific producers themselves. Perhaps most important are the courses of schools, colleges, and universities, and their associated textbooks and laboratories. In these settings the scientist is clearly dominant over his clientele; he repeatedly evaluates their performance, and his evaluations of them are far more consequential than their evaluations of him.

Scientists also control, in large part, the media of printed communication, of which the journals are the most important segment. Among other things, this entails that they are almost assured that what they write will be published. Although average journal rejection rates range from 24% in physics to 84% in political science (Zuckerman and Merton, 1971: 76), scientists can submit articles repeatedly, and initial rejection rarely prevents the eventual publication of a manuscript (Garvey and Griffith, 1971: 358). In addition, many articles have extremely few readers. For example, it has been estimated that about half of the research reports in the core journals of psychology are likely to be read by less than 1 percent (or two hundred) psychologists (Garvey and Griffity, 1971: 358). Even if read, papers may never be referred to; a study of the papers published in the major journal of a subfield of physics showed that 10% of those published in 1967-1968 were never referred to in the succeeding seven years (Gillmore, 1975)! Clearly, "marketability" is not the primary criterion in the decision to publish.

Scientists spend a large fraction of their time evaluating the work of others. Most academic scientists serve as journal referees at one time or another. About 12% of the scientists in my 1966 survey had been editors or associate editors of journals, and more than one-quarter had served on advisory committees for governmental or other research funding agencies. In addition, academic scientists spend much time evaluating the work of students and candidates for appointments and promotions. This relatively great attention devoted to evaluating the work of others may be typical of culture producers in all fields. For example, Batia Sharon (1969) surveyed an inclusive sample of Chicago artists and found that a majority had served as jurors for art shows, more than one-third of them doing so at least four times in their careers.

The common small readership of articles in scientific journals suggests that they often serve primarily as communication channels for the network clusters I have described above. The meetings of scientific societies also have this as a major function. Network clusters also involve frequent, less formal communication. For example, Hargens (1975: 29) found that academic chemists report spending an average of more than four hours per week on professional correspondence; and 62% attended professional meetings, of one sort or another, for at least six days a year. In tightly knit clusters, informal communication is much more frequent and intensive.

If journals often serve the interests of network clusters, they are also accessible to anyone else with the qualifications to read them. Thus, the literature in all the fields of basic science is linked by references from papers in each field to papers in often quite dissimilar other fields. The literature in basic science is also potentially accessible to applied scientists and engineers. However, studies of the communication behavior of engineers show that they seldom use the literature of the basic sciences (Marquis and Allen, 1966; Allen, 1970). Often that literature is written in a language they cannot understand, and often they cannot search the basic literature to find what they need to know. Thus, references in patents are usually to other patents, and references in applied science and engineering journals are usually to the same types of journals. Unlike basic scientists, engineers tend to be oriented less to external communication than to the unpublished technical reports of their employing organizations and to interpersonal contacts within these organizations. Given this typical internal orientation, it is not surprising that Allen (1970) found that a small number of gatekeepers played a critical role in transferring scientific and technical information across the organizational boundaries to development groups within. These gatekeepers tended to be scientists and engineers who were well-educated, more widely read, and maintained closer personal ties with persons outside the firm. In addition to such gatekeepers, personal consultation with academic scientists plays an important role in transferring information from basic science to technology; direct consultation reduces the costs of search and permits the negotiation of mutually comprehensible languages. Despite criticisms of the speed and extent to which basic research is brought to bear on societal needs, and despite considerable interindustry variability, the loose links between science and technology seem to have been remarkably effective in recent decades (Nelson and Pollock, 1970).

The preceding paragraphs have stressed the dissemination of scientific knowledge among professionals and have neglected the dissemination of such knowledge in the larger lay community. This reflects the recent research interests of sociologists of science, who have paid far less attention to folk culture or mass culture than have sociologists of art, music, or religion. However, research by anthropologists of ethnoscience suggests that modern science (among other things) has had deep and extensive effects on the belief systems of persons in developed societies. Comparative studies of developed and developing societies show that children and adults in the former are much more able than those in the latter to cope with abstract problems, present coherent explanations of a range of natural phenomena, and recognize the possibility that knowledge may be obtained from empirical research instead of from traditional authorities alone (see, e.g., Gay and Cole, 1967; Dart and Pradhan, 1967).

The same studies show that persons in developing nations often have a kind of dualistic belief system, asserting the "validity" of both Western school-based knowledge and apparently inconsistent traditional beliefs. For example, Nepalese school children readily assert the truth of both the propositions that "Lightning comes from the collision of clouds," and "Lightning comes from the bangles of Indra's dancers" (Dart and Pradhan, 1967: 651). Persons in developed societies are much less likely to have such a duality of viewpoint. This does not imply that the scientific culture of the professionals is accepted without question by persons in developed societies. Laymen can recognize that professionals may have different goals and interests than themselves, and they may discount the teaching and advice of professionals after taking such differences into account. The process is nicely illustrated in Becker's (1974) comparison of how the effects of drugs are assessed when the situation is controlled by users, by users' agents (e.g., physicians and pharmaceutical companies), and by external agents (e.g., professional staff in mental hospitals); the main and side effects of drugs may be assessed quite differently in the three situations. While Becker stresses the different *rationalities* of laymen and professionals, other types of lay rejection of orthodox science may require closer study of the expressive significance of deviant beliefs. The popular science distributed in mass media, such as newspaper Sunday supplements, the *National Enquirer,* or women's magazines, often emphasizes such unorthodox approaches as parapsychology, astrology, or variants of flying saucer stories. We do not know how important such beliefs are in modern societies; explanation of their significance may be as much the task of the sociologist of religion as the sociologist of science.

In any case, scientists engaged in teaching, or whose work depends on the actions of political leaders, can be quite aware of the reluctance of laymen to admit that the knowledge they seek to offer is either relevant or valid. Lay skepticism may be a function of such factors as the cost, in money or consumer effort, to acquire the knowledge; the degree to which orthodox science deviates from common sense; the relation of scientists to dominant institutions; and the degree of consensus among culture producers. It is reasonable to believe that lay skepticism will erode the authority of scientists and societal support for scientific research.

## TRANSFORMATIONS OF SCIENTIFIC CULTURE

Unlike many commodities, culture can be consumed without destroying it: culture is not like cake. In fact, the "consumption" of culture in the classroom, theater, or elsewhere, can mean its "reproduction." Nevertheless, scientific products are, if not destroyed, revolutionized, surpassed, and abandoned. The metaphor of the production of culture can help understand such processes to some extent. For example, just as rapid change leads to the obsolescence of commodities, it can lead to the obsolescence of knowledge and those scientists and technical workers possessing that knowledge. Such obsolescence has been perceived as problematic by social science students or engineers and employers of engineers. Engineers are most likely to become obsolete if they have worked in a relatively routine area that becomes rapidly changed by new discoveries; they are less likely to become obsolete if they have advanced degrees and work in areas of advanced and nonroutine technology (Perrucci and Rothman, 1969).

A related kind of transformation in science is the "exhaustion" of research opportunities in a specialty (cf. Crane, 1972). This may occur when workers in a field find difficulty in discovering interesting problems for research that can be approached with existing techniques. The obligation to do research that is both original and interesting tends to force workers to change specialties; preparing for research in a new specialty may be burdensome and risky, carrying no assurance of success, and some scientists abandon active research rather than take such risks. More generally, the difficulty of finding intrinsically important research problems may lead to "fashions" in science—scientists may select problems because others do, rather than because of any personal conviction in the importance of the problem (Hagstrom, 1965: 177-184). Crane (1969) has argued that such behavior, considered deviant by scientists, is actually uncommon.

More radical transformations in scientific culture are not so readily interpreted with the production-of-culture metaphor. Since the appearance of Thomas Kuhn's *The Structure of Scientific Revolutions* in 1962, thought about such transformations has been more heavily influenced by political metaphors. Such a contrast between production and political metaphors may do justice to neither, however. Many others have recognized that not only the production of culture, but the production of other goods, requires consideration of concepts and theories about political behavior and collective behavior.

## REFERENCES

ALLEN, T. J. (1970) "Roles in technical communication networks," pp. 191-208 in C. E. Nelson and D. K. Pollock (eds.) Communication Among Scientists and Engineers. Lexington, Mass.: D. C. Heath.

BECKER, H. S. (1974) "Consciousness, power and drug effects." J. of Psychedelic Drugs 6 (January-March): 67-76.

COLLINS, R. (1975) Conflict Sociology: Toward an Explanatory Science. New York: Academic.

CRANE, D. (1972) Invisible Colleges: Diffusion of Knowledge in Scientific Communities. Chicago: Univ. of Chicago Press.

––– (1969) "Fashion in science: does it exist?" Social Problems 16 (Spring): 433-441.

CROWTHER, J. G. (1935) British Scientists of the Nineteenth Century. London: Routledge & Kegan Paul.

DART, F. E. and P. L. PRADHAN (1967) "Cross-cultural teaching of science." Science 155 (10 February): 649-656.

FISHER, C. S. (1973) "Some social characteristics of mathematicians and their work." Amer. J. of Sociology 78: 1094-1118.

GARVEY, W. D. and B. C. GRIFFITH (1971) "Scientific communication: its role in the conduct of research and creation of knowledge." Amer. Psychologist 26 (April): 349-362.

GAY, J. and M. COLE (1967) The New Mathematics and an Old Culture: A Study of Learning Among the Kpelle of Liberia. New York: Holt, Rinehart & Winston.

GILLMORE, C. S. (1975) "Citation characteristics of the JATP literature." J. of Atmospheric & Terrestrial Physics (in press).

GRANOVETTER, M. S. (1973) "The strength of weak ties." Amer. J. of Sociology 78 (May): 1360-1380.

GRIFFITH, B. and A. J. MILLER (1970) "Networks of informal communication among scientifically productive scientists," pp. 125-140 in C. E. Nelson and D. K. Pollock (eds.) Communication Among Scientists and Engineers. Lexington, Mass.: D. C. Heath.

HAGSTROM, W. O. (1974) "Competition in science." Amer. Soc. Rev. 39 (February): 1-18.

––– (1967) "Competition and teamwork in science." Final report to the National

Science Foundation for research grant GS-657, University of Wisconsin, Madison. (mimeo).

——— (1965) The Scientific Community. New York: Basic Books.

——— (1964) "Anomy in scientific organizations." Social Problems 12 (Fall): 186-195.

HARGENS, L. L. (1975) Patterns of Scientific Research. Washington, D.C.: American Sociological Association.

KAPLAN, A. (1964) The Conduct of Inquiry. San Francisco: Chandler.

KUHN, T. S. (1970) The Structure of Scientific Revolutions, second ed. Chicago: Univ. of Chicago Press.

LAKATOS, I. and A. MUSGRAVE (1970) "Criticism and the growth of knowledge." Proceedings of the International Colloquium in the Philosophy of Science, London, 1965, Vol. 4. Cambridge: Cambridge Univ. Press.

MARCH, J. G. and H. SIMON (1958) Organizations. New York: John Wiley.

MARQUIS, D. G. and T. J. ALLEN (1966) "Communication patterns in applied technology." Amer. Psychologist 21: 1052-1060.

MAYHEW, G. P. (1967) "Recent Swift scholarship," pp. 187-197 in R. McHugh and P. Edwards (eds.) Johnathan Swift 1667-1967. Dublin: Dolman.

NELSON, C. E. and D. K. POLLOCK (1970) Communication Among Scientists and Engineers. Lexington, Mass. D. C. Heath.

PERROW, C. (1972) Complex Organizations: A Critical Essay. Glenview, Ill.: Scott, Foresman.

——— (1967) "A framework for the comparative analysis of organizations." Amer. Soc. Rev. 32 (April): 194-208.

PERRUCCI, R. and R. A. ROTHMAN (1969) "Obsolescence of knowledge and the professional career," pp. 247-276 in R. Perrucci and J. E. Gersel (eds.) The Engineers and the Social System. New York: John Wiley.

Philological Quarterly (1974) Vol. 53 (Fall): 802-807.

PRICE, D. J. de S. (1963) Little Science, Big Science. New York: Columbia Univ. Press.

RITTI, R. R. and F. H. GOLDNER (1969) "Professional pluralism in an industrial organization." Management Sci. 16 (December): B-233-B-246.

SHARON, B. (1969) "Center and periphery in Chicago's art community." Master's thesis, University of Wisconsin, Department of Sociology.

STINCHCOMBE, A. L. (1966) "On getting 'hung-up' and other assorted illnesses." Johns Hopkins Mag. (Winter): 25-30.

SULLIVAN, D., D. H. WHITE and E. BARBONI (1975) "The state of a science: indicators in the specialty of weak interactions." Delivered at the annual meeting of the American Sociological Association, San Francisco.

SWATEZ, G. M. (1970) "The social organization of a university laboratory." Minerva 8 (January): 36-58.

WOODWARD, J. (1965) Industrial Organization: Theory and Practice. London: Oxford Univ. Press.

ZUCKERMAN, H. and R. K. MERTON (1971) "Patterns of evaluation in science: institutionalization, structure and functions of the referee system." Minerva 9: 66-100.

*Kadushin uses network analysis to show the distinctive structure of intellectual, scientific, and artistic circles. These circles of creators are contrasted with the utilitarian production networks which transfer creations into consumables.*

# Networks and Circles in the Production of Culture

CHARLES KADUSHIN
*Teachers College*
*Columbia University*

**One of the latest catchwords** in social science is "network." A network is a set of social objects onto which is mapped a set of relationships or "flows" not necessarily in a 1:1 fashion. This idea has been around for a long time (Barnes, 1972), but it has recently been taken less metaphorically and more seriously. It has inspired a number of theoretically interesting studies of events in a wide variety of settings.[1] Network analysis obviously possesses in large measure a major virtue of any approach in social science—versatility. In this paper I propose to test some of this versatility by applying the concept to studies of the production of culture.

Networks have been frequently identified with informal or what might be called "emergent" relations—those which are not formally instituted. Of course, role and status sets are also fit subjects for network analysis, for they too are networks.

**Author's Note:** *This paper was prepared under a grant to the author by the National Science Foundation. It is part of a series of studies of networks of leaders at the Bureau of Applied Social Research and in other centers in other countries. See Barton et al. (1973), Barton (1974), Moore (1974), Higley et al. (1975), Kadushin and Rose (1974), and Neumann et al. (1973). I gratefully acknowledge the help given by Richard A. Peterson and other participants in the Production of Culture Symposium.*

Nonetheless, in discussing the production of culture, I shall emphasize emergent networks because they are especially apt for this field. In addition, emergent networks tend to be less visible than formally instituted networks. Emergent networks in the area of culture production also tend to be interstitial—that is, tend to link different social units such as different universities, publishers, authors, and the like. These kinds of connections also seem more dramatic than, for example, clique relations within the same structure, although both are network phenomena. The degree to which networks are instituted or emergent, visible or less visible, interstitial or not defines networks of different types. Our concern here is with the very special kind of network which is emergent, is by and large interstitial, whose visibility is generally relatively low, and which is a *macro-phenomenon* (see McPhee, 1963; Kadushin, 1975; and Tichy, 1976), not a micro one. These networks are typical of culture production systems.

**CIRCLES**

Producers of culture are also consumers. The flow through producer networks is, therefore, at least two-way and often circular. Most intellectuals, writers, painters, actors, musicians, and poets are avid consumers of each other's performances. For example, the average respondent in my study of elite American intellectuals (Kadushin, 1974) checked off 14 journals of general content as his monthly reading fare. In fact, the circular relationship between performer and audience has been instituted in the citation system of science: all performers must demonstrate that they have read other performers' work. The major formal problem for students of networks who wish to apply what is known about diffusion to studies of the production of culture is the circularity of a system in which each member is an opinion leader who influences other opinion leaders through an N-step process. The generic form of the network of producers is therefore the social circle.

Circles have some distinct properties, ones which often prove puzzling to observers and which make circles emergent, low visibility, interstitial networks. First, circles have *no clear boundaries*, and the dividing line between the center and the periphery is often arbitrarily drawn. Because the boundary lines are not especially clear and because any individual member of a circle can "see" only his immediate surrounding contacts, "natives" of circles frequently have only fuzzy, if not totally incorrect, notions of what their circle looks like. Thus, American elite intellectuals had widely varying impressions of American intellectual circles, and most of these descriptions were wrong (Kadushin, 1974: ch. 3).

The second structural property of a circle, *indirect interaction*, means that not everyone has to know everyone else or have contact with everyone else. The flow of symbols or objects may be via one or two others, on the average, as well as directly from one person to another.[2] The circle is viable even if most members do not relate directly to most other members. In this respect, it is quite different from a group.

A further structural characteristic of circles is that they often have a *core of even greater density* than the rest of the circle, or sometimes several such cores, *but no formal leadership.* In the circles of intellectuals we studied, there were indeed some members who were more central than others, but even Richard Kostelanetz (1974) would have difficulty in saying "Take me to your leader."

A fourth characteristic of a circle is its relative *lack of instituted structures and norms*–that is, their "emergent" character. Like the face-to-face "informal organizations" which reside within more formally constituted organizations, circles lack clear norms about structure, leadership, membership, modes of interrelationships between members, and overall goal or purpose. This does not mean that individual sets of members who relate to one another do not know why they do so. On the contrary, circles arise to solve the problems of individual members who relate to one another because they have certain common interests and needs. It is the "organization" as a whole that lacks a purpose for, after all, in common with most other networks, *circles are invisible in their totality,* and this invisibility is their fifth major characteristic.

A sixth characteristic of circles, and this they have in common with other influence nets, is that because they are not instituted, they are always "pegged to" or "draped around" other structures. That is, the lines of influence or interaction tend to follow other more formal relations, whether it be common occupational status or some relationship to a formal organization such as an intellectual journal, a theater group, a gallery, or even a bar or cafe. A major research task in the study of cultural networks is to discover the relationship between the more formal networks and the less formal ones. More restrictedly, this has been called the "homophily problem" (Lazarsfeld and Merton, 1954).

Finally, circles in the cultural field are all the manifestation of the fact that culture production is an *external economy industry* (Vernon, 1963)—that is, an industry whose production line includes factors that are available only outside of the individual production organization. This is what makes cultural networks interstitial. A typical example given by economists is the women's high fashion garment industry. This is an industry characterized by a large number of fairly small producers huddled together in their mutual dependence upon designers, each other (for "stealing" ideas), specialty suppliers (of buttons, cloth, and so on), and a flexible labor supply of specialists who drift in and out of being workers or subcontractors. Other external economy industries are Wall Street, advertising, radio-TV, music, film, publishing, theater, and art. The circle is the structural form taken by most relations in external economy industries.

The kind of information which flows through circles is a useful basis for defining types of circles. There are four kinds of interests which circle members may have in common (Kadushin, 1968: 692): utilitarian, power and influence, integration, and, of course, cultural—our major concern here. Utilitarian circles such as "Wall Street" are characterized by the need to trade goods and services with other producers and are the origin of the theory of "external economy" industries (Vernon, 1963). Political power and influence circles, which we have elsewhere called "interaction sets" (Kadushin, 1975), are those involved in studies of local and national elite systems. Neither of these two types of circles is necessarily characterized by value homophily. Integrative circles specialize in affect flow and, on the macro-level, result from the elaboration of a common experience such as ethnic membership, wartime experience, or membership in an occupational community. We will not be further concerned here with utilitarian, power-influence, and integrative circles except insofar as cultural circles include them as secondary themes.

Different types of cultural circles roughly correspond to the different domains of culture. Circles which emphasize values, esthetics, ideology, and religion generally have the form of "intellectual circles." Those which emphasize expressive concerns such as literature, art, and music often take the form of a "movement circle," while those with cognitive emphases have been called "invisible colleges" (Price, 1963, Crane, 1972). Since the production of culture is also a market phenomenon in large-scale consumer society, there are also cultural networks (if not circles) which emphasize utilitarian concerns, and these are "journeyman" and "brokerage" nets. Finally, there are networks of "audiences" or "consumers" which, due to space limitations, will not be discussed here.[3] These circles and networks differ in their structural characteristics, the degree to which they are pegged to different formal structures as well as the nature of these pegs, and their flows and functions. They also tend to move through different phases of development. Since the investigation of cultural circles is in its infancy, much of what I shall say about them in declarative form must be taken as tentative propositions, poorly grounded in data.

## INTELLECTUAL CIRCLES

Let me begin with intellectual circles, for we know more about them than others (Kadushin, 1974; Coser, 1965), especially because intellectuals are persons of the word, and so they like to write about, among other things, themselves. Unlike any of the other circles of culture producers with which we shall deal, intellectual circles are networks of generalists and therefore often tend to cross occupational lines. Intellectuals, of the kind we are talking about, produce ideas about values, morals, politics, and esthetics, not for specialists but for so-called educated laymen and, of course, for each other. The intellectual himself may have his own academic specialty, be it nineteenth-century literature, baroque art, or social stratification. But ideas produced for the general marketplace can neither be stimulated nor evaluated by the usual professional networks. A major function of the intellectual circles, therefore, is to evaluate both the ideas and the persons who produce them. Proof of this function is seen in the absence of circles. Clark (1973) shows that when intellectual "clusters," as he calls them, remain essentially centered around a single Patron rather than encompassing a wider group, intellectual quality deteriorates. And the current state of poor health of American intellectual journals is in part caused by the general weakening of the structure of American intellectual circles as a result of the trauma of the 1960s and the counter-culture.

Modern intellectual circles developed after the growth of modern complex societies made the salon too limited a means for intellectual exchange. Coffee houses or bars as meeting places around which circles are formed abound in intellectual history. Both geography and having been to the same schools at the same time is important—as, for example, in the Bloomsbury circle. Common political activity and views have been and remain important. The literary-political journal of general interest, a device "invented" by some Scottish intellectuals in the early nineteenth century (the *Edinburgh Review*), is an especially important peg in societies with some geographic dispersion of intellectuals, as is the case for the contemporary United States (and, of course, England and Scotland of the nineteenth century). Book publishers, at least in the United States, now do not seem to work well as intellectual circle "pegs," although they might have done so in earlier times. Occupation and even current university faculty membership, although they count, do not seem as important in the United States, at least, as some other pegs, although religious origin is probably more important than we first thought.

All the factors mentioned above do relate to the "homophily" of intellectual relations in the United States (Alba and Kadushin, 1976). From what I know impressionistically about other countries, geography is extremely important, if only negatively because, except for the United States, almost all the intellectuals who count live in the capital city. Political party activity and views are also quite important in Europe. The meeting place is also more important in Europe than in the United States for in some countries, if one sat daily in a select set of cafes or restaurants, one might garner a good sample of the intellectual elite, a circle much less specialized in occupation than in the United States. In most European countries, writers, professors, editors, and free-lance intellectuals of one kind or another mingle with artists, theater and film persons, and musicians. In the United States, intellectual, theater, film and music circles seem to overlap only slightly. American geographic dispersion may well account for this pattern, but so may our relative lack of interest in politics and world views, together with our strong careerism, which tends to produce a narrow occupational focus.

Intellectual circles may well be subject to "social lag." The circles in the United States that I studied reflected interests, ideas, politics and friendships of some ten years' or so standing, at the minimum, and represented the way cold war issues had been resolved in the late 1950s. The "new" issue of the time, the war in Vietnam, for various reasons, did not restructure these older circles. Rather than discussion of the war following the existing circle pattern, word diffused from a central core composed of "experts" on the topic. Other structural pegs were less important. It is hard to say whether these findings are typical, but at least they are plausible and the only systematic case we have. If we were to generalize, we would speculate that circles, even as ephemeral as they are, are nonetheless tied to existing social structures which are, in turn, tied to many other structures and values.

Relationships bound to such structures are not so easy to break. An effective intellectual system does, however, allow new ideas to be transmitted, even though they are evaluated along the structural lines (and, perforce, the ideology) of old circles. Eventually, either the disparity between the ideas and the circles grows intolerable, or else a new generation with new ties enters, together with new ideas, and forms a new pattern of circles. But the death and transfiguration of circles remain topics with little hard research data.

## CIRCLES IN SCIENCE

The relation of social structure to new ideas is clearer in areas in which the growth of ideas tends to be specialized, cumulative, and exponential. Such is the case with science (Merton, 1973). Crane (1972) argues that the periods of rapid growth in science stem in part from personal influence on the selection of problems. There is evidence that such influence follows the familiar two-step flow found in diffusion studies. Social circles in science, or invisible colleges, tend to abound in such periods. Conversely, fields of scientific work which have little informal social structure tend to be fields which have either passed their period of rapid growth and are no longer "hot" or have not yet come into such a period. The lack of informal social structure may, therefore, actually impede the development of a field—further verifying the function of circles.

While Crane and others tend to stress the informational content of scientific networks, evaluation and exhortation—leading to "taste"—are also very important. Thus, circles in science arise not only to circulate information in a new field—information that by definition is not yet available in print, but also to support the new ideas and to encourage self-awareness among scientists that their current endeavors have a unique place. For unlike intellectual circles which dedifferentiate in order to produce scientific knowledge, scientific circles grow from the need to specialize and differentiate in order to produce scientific knowledge.

The structural form taken by circles in science seems, on the basis of several studies (Price, 1965; Griffith and Mullins, 1972; Mullins, 1968; Crane, 1972, and those cited by her) to be somewhat different than that of intellectual circles. While there are many intellectual "stars," concentration on a small set of stars seems more pronounced in scientific circles. The pattern, which does vary somewhat from field to field, seems to be that of a number of relatively tight groups composed of current and past collaborators on research and current and former master-student relations.[4] Current or past propinquity seems important for these groups (as it is for intellectual circles). The groups, when they interact with other groups, tend to do so via the "stars," who in turn interact with each other as well as with members of their own group. There are really two sets of circles, therefore, in most active scientific communities (excluding those who do not publish much): a large set of clumps or clusters centered around stars and, at the core of the entire system, an "elite invisible college" which directly links the stars. For this latter circle, propinquity is unimportant.

The basic differences between invisible college systems (as a generic term for scientific circles) and intellectual circles lie in the nature of their "external economies." Most of the work of elite intellectuals is noncollaborative and, for that matter, largely noncumulative (Aristotle is as good a reference as Arendt). They depend on interaction for stimulation and for idea-testing, but not for idea production. Most scientists work in teams and are frequently (though much less than business executive teams) part of the same formal organization. Nonetheless, if a team remains isolated, the content of its ideas and its productivity are both likely to suffer. Elite scientists probably depend on contact with other elite scientists as much as do elite intellectuals, however, and their circles are likely not only to be cross-institutional but also cross-national. Elite as well as nonelite scientists depend on other scientists for ideas, which are often in written form (but in quickly growing fields not formally printed), thus making it possible even for the nonelite to have "contact" with the elite. This need for contact on the "leading edge" in a rapidly growing field is an important aspect of the external economy of science.

Cognitive matters are not the only flow through the channels of scientific and intellectual exchange. Money and other rewards flow, too. Unlike elite intellectuals (who until very recently could at best hope for a Guggenheim Fellowship or its equivalent once or twice in a lifetime), elite scientists are perpetually in the business of raising large sums of money for research. This activity in itself creates an external economy network of grantees and recipients who, because of the peer review system, are likely to change places with the regularity of a musical chairs game. Just what effect the informal structure of science has on the granting business is a touchy subject and, therefore, it has not been systematically explored, although there have been studies of the formal affiliations of grantees and grantors (Mullins, 1972). The functional equivalent in the intellectual world is the reviewing system often described (Kostelanetz, 1974) as venal and parochial, in which circle members review each other's works favorably (or at the very least review them, rather than letting them die through the censorship of neglect), but the system seems less structured than the grant system.[5] Finally, peer review in science for books, articles, and grant applications is also more systematically structured. Here, too, the operation of networks of reviewers and reviewees has not been directly studied though Zuckerman and Merton (1971) have developed data which suggest that particularism is not an important factor in the judgments about manuscripts submitted to the *Physical Review.*

Last, but hardly least, the job market in both scientific and intellectual circles also operates through networks established for other purposes. One suspects that scientific circles are more effective than intellectual circles in securing full-time jobs for members, since being a scientist is an occupation, while being a general intellectual is not. The network of intellectuals does, however, allocate among its members book contracts, magazine assignments, reviews, lectures, and the like, involving important amounts of money even to those intellectuals (the majority) who have steady jobs. Although there is much myth about the importance of word of mouth in getting jobs and assignments, one careful study (Granovetter, 1974) shows that, despite the importance of networks, the more *distant* contacts are more useful to the individual than the more proximate ones, because the distant contacts are privy to information that one's immediate circle does not have.

In sum, intellectual and scientific circles have somewhat different external economies, and this tends to produce circles of differing structure. A basic issue for further research is the relationship of the primary idea flows in intellectual and scientific circles to subsidiary utilitarian flows such as money and other rewards, power and influence flows—the "politics" of intellectual life and scientific circles, and integrative flows via occupational community.

## MOVEMENT CIRCLES[6]

Partisanship is well known in scientific and intellectual circles, but there is a pretense of inclusiveness and universality. Since the Romantic movement in the nineteenth century, however, poetry, fiction, painting, theater, and music have often been self-consciously parochial, with producers of culture huddling together in "movements." We have neither the space nor the hard data to discuss movement circles in detail, but a few speculative observations may throw intellectual and scientific circles into relief. The kind of movement circle we have in mind is typified by the New York Action School in art or the alternative or experimental theater movement (e.g., Open Theater) in drama. Kostelanetz (1974) describes similar movements in poetry and literature.

Movement circles emphasize creativity as do scientific and intellectual circles, but movement circles also tend to create "against" some established principles or images. It is the sense of embattlement that leads to common bonding. If we had quantitative data, it might well be that the average network distance between any pair in movement circles would be less than in cultural and scientific circles. The controversial nature of movement circles also seems to lend to them a more *obvious* life cycle or natural history than is the case for the other circles. The first stage is divided into two phases. In the first or start-up phase, the circle is very inclusive. Anyone who is "on our side" may join, and the typical linkage is through friends with no particular questions asked. In the second phase of the first stage, the circle becomes more concerned with boundary clarity, and members attempt, within the limitation of circle diffuseness of style, to fix the notion of "membership." Some persons may join, but others may not; some are expelled while others stay. This greater structural rigidity goes hand in hand with an attempt to give the ideas of the movement greater artistic clarity.

In the second stage, the nascent circle has become itself a kind of "establishment." The first phase of the second stage continues the emphasis on standards of belonging, but the standards are now more abstract and less ad hominem as they begin to become codified. The circle now more clearly has a central core and a periphery. In the final phase, the circle is now itself an "establishment" and has instituted forms or organizations or journals upon which the circle drapes itself. The circle may even come to have official university status and connections. It is now ripe for a new rebellion against its authority. Only at this last stage is the movement circle nongeographic and less dependent on propinquity. The urban milieu described by Simmel (1950, 1955—originally, 1902 and 1922) of overlapping circles well describes the social, artistic, and intellectual "external economy" of movement circles and explains why they as well as the more inclusive intellectual circles are almost always found in a country's major metropolis, at least when circles are in their most fruitful and growing phases (Craven and Wellman, 1973; Fischer, 1975).

## UTILITARIAN NETWORKS IN CULTURE PRODUCTION

Finally, we have the journeyman net and the brokerage net. Neither of these are circles in the sense of having a clearly defined dense region or core, although obviously some parts of the net are more dense than others. In these nets what was secondary to circles of culture production—utilitarian concerns—becomes primary, and what was primary—the production of culture—becomes secondary. A journeyman net is typified by the seemingly chaotic pattern of job-finding in the performing arts, including music, and the process of socialization to the occupational community (Kadushin, 1969b). Journeymen, actors, and musicians are linked in rather long nets in terms of the need to find jobs: being professional means participation in such nets and holding paying jobs at least at union scale. Academic standards tend to be downgraded in favor of action and "doing." Much more needs to be said about such systems, their "pegs," and other characteristics, but that discussion will have to be reserved for other occasions.

An investigation into the role of publishers as gatekeepers of ideas is currently being undertaken by Lewis Coser, myself, and Woody Powell (see Hirsch, 1972; Boissevain, 1974; Coser, 1975). It is premature to report any conclusions, but it does appear that publishers occupy a position in book-producing like that of the foreman in industrial plants. They are the persons in the middle, linking producers of culture with both the market of sources of capital and the market of consumers. The best ones blend in their soul all three worlds—capital, audience, and culture producer. It turns out that there are layers and layers of brokers in publishing, just as there are in the theater, music, and the art market: publishers, book editors, author's agents, and more. Within the world of publishing, there are different circles, corresponding in part, but not entirely, to the kind of book published and the way it is marketed. Rumor, word of mouth, and contacts count almost for everything. Indeed, publishers have institutionalized a major social ritual—eating—as one of their major occasions for making contacts and thus doing their business as a way of symbolizing the importance of social contact. Again, this topic must be fully explored elsewhere.

In conclusion, this paper can only allude to the most vexing problem of the sociology of knowledge—the relationship of social structure to the content and style of ideas—by noting that the main point of this paper has been to show how the systematic study of the properties of different social circles affects and is affected by the content and style of the ideas produced by members of the circle. Whether a firm relationship between content and form can be further substantiated, and whether an adequate theory can be developed to account for existing findings and to predict future ones, remain to be seen.[7]

## NOTES

1. This wide range is exemplified by friendship patterns in Malta (Boissevain, 1974), the Mafia in the United States (Ianni, 1972, 1974) and in Sicily (Blok, 1974), mining in Africa (Kapferer, 1969), leisure patterns in England (Bott, 1971), job-searching in America (Granovetter, 1974), the search for psychiatric help in New York City (Kadushin, 1966, 1969a), corporate overlap in the Netherlands (Mokken and Stokman, 1974) and the United States (Sonquist and Koenig, 1975), elite studies, and many more.

2. Some chains are long—having as many as 15 steps. In data we have seen, however, the magic number seems to be an average of two or three steps for most circles (Pool, 1973). An algorithm for clustering circles generally, therefore, has to consider only those persons one or two steps away from any ego (Alba and Kadushin, 1976).

3. Audiences do not in fact depend only on the evaluations of culture producers; rather, at least some members of the audience, called opinion leaders, actively participate in passing around the objects and symbols which originate at the center (Lazarsfeld et al., 1944). Most movie-goers evaluate new films as much on the basis of

their friends' opinions as they do on mass media hype; voters are at least as much influenced by other voters as they are by the campaign (Katz and Lazarsfeld, 1955); most physicians prescribe new drugs only after their friends have done so, whatever they may have previously read about the drug (Coleman et al., 1966); and the same is true for the adoption of contraceptives (Katz, 1957) or new agricultural techniques (Rogers and Shoemaker, 1971). This pattern generally operates in one direction— from producer to consumer. In most audience studies, therefore, symbols or objects which pass through the network are regarded as immutable, at least for most purposes. Of course, audiences do affect performances, but in general audiences do not produce new symbols or objects.

4. The data must be regarded as tentative, since recent techniques which objectively partition large networks had not been developed at the time these studies were published. See Roistacher (1974).

5. One reason for the lack of structure in intellectual reviewing is that its effect is less directly financial than scientific reviewing. As Crane (1972) points out, scientists themselves tend to control all of their rewards, whereas the penumbra of intellectual circles and the mass market control much of the financial if not the artistic rewards of intellectual generalists. The extent to which good or bad reviews affect this market is at least questionable.

6. This section has profited from discussions with Rhea Gaisner and others of the "Open Theater." Diana Crane suggests that movement circles also occur in scientific fields.

7. A promising theory has been advanced by Ekeh (1974) and is more fully described elsewhere (Kadushin, 1975). In essence, it tries to elaborate some ideas of Levi-Strauss and show that certain kinds of network patternings produce certain kinds of ideology, but that takes us even further afield.

# REFERENCES

ALBA, R. D. and C. KADUSHIN (1976) "The intersection of social circles: a new measure of social proximity in networks." Sociological Methods and Research (August).

BARNES, J. A. (1972) Social Networks. Reading, Mass.: Addison-Wesley Module in Anthropology 26.

BARTON, A. H. (1974) "Consensus and conflict among American leaders." Public Opinion Q. 38 (Winter): 507-530.

——— B. DENITCH, AND C. KADUSHIN (1973) Opinion-Making Elites in Yugoslavia. New York: Praeger.

BLOK, A. (1974) The Mafia of a Sicilian Village, 1860-1960. New York: Harper & Row.

BOISSEVAIN, J. (1974) Friends of Friends: Networks, Manipulators and Coalitions. Oxford: Basil Blackwell.

——— and J. C. MITCHELL (1973) Network Analysis: Studies in Human Interaction. The Hague: Mouton.

BOTT, E. (1971) Family and Social Network, second ed. New York: Free Press. (first ed., 1957)

CLARK, T. N. (1973) Prophets and Patrons: The French University and the Emergence of the Social Sciences. Cambridge: Harvard Univ. Press.

COLEMAN, J., E. KATZ, and H. MENZEL (1966) Medical Innovation: A Diffusion Study. Indianapolis: Bobbs-Merrill.

COSER, L. (1975) "Publishers as gatekeepers of ideas." Annals of the Amer. Academy of Pol. & Social Sci. 421 (September): 14-22.

——— (1965) Men of Ideas. New York: Free Press.

CRANE, D. (1972) Invisible Colleges: Diffusion of Knowledge in Scientific Communities. Chicago: Univ. of Chicago Press.

CRAVEN, P. and B. WELLMAN (1973) "The network city." Soc. Inquiry 43 (December): 57-88.

DUNCAN, H. D. (1964) The Rise of Chicago as a Literary Center from 1885 to 1920. Totowa, N.J.: Bedminster.

EKEH, P. P. (1974) Social Exchange Theory: The Two Traditions. Cambridge: Harvard Univ. Press.

FIELD, G. L. (1973) Elites and Non-Elites: Their Possibilities and Some Side Effects. Andover, Mass.: Warner Module No. 13.

FISCHER, C. S. (1975) "Toward a subcultural theory of urbanism." Amer. J. of Sociology 80: 1319-1341.

GRANOVETTER, M. S. (1974) Getting a Job: A Study of Contacts and Careers. Cambridge: Harvard Univ. Press.

GRIFFITH, B. C. and N. C. MULLINS (1972) "Coherent social groups in scientific change: 'invisible colleges' may be consistent throughout science." Science 177 (15 September): 959-964.

HIGLEY, J., G. L. FIELD, and K. GROHOLT (1975) Elite Structure and Ideology in Developed Societies: A Theoretical Study of National Elites in Norway. New York: Columbia Univ. Press.

HIRSCH, P. M. (1972) "Processing fads and fashions: an organization set analysis of cultural industry systems." Amer. J. of Sociology 77 (January): 639-659.

IANNI, F.A.J. (1974) Black Mafia. New York: Simon & Schuster.

——— (1972) A Family Business. New York: Russell Sage.

KADUSHIN, C. (1975) "Introduction to the sociological study of networks." (unpublished mss.)

——— (1974) The American Intellectual Elite. Boston: Little, Brown.

——— (1969a) Why People Go to Psychiatrists. New York: Atherton.

——— (1969b) "The professional self-concept of music students." Amer. J. of Sociology 75 (September): 389-404.

——— (1968) "Power, influence and social circles: a new methodology for studying opinion-makers." Amer. Soc. Rev. 33 (February): 685-699.

——— (1966) "The friends and supporters of psychotherapy: on social circles in urban life." Amer. Soc. Rev. 31 (December): 786-802.

——— and R. ROSE (1974) "Recent developments in comparative political sociology: determinates of electoral behavior and the structure of elite networks," pp. 229-266 in Current Research in Sociology. The Hague: Mouton.

KAPFERER, B. (1969) "Norms and the manipulation of relationships in a work context," pp. 181-244 in J. C. Mitchell (ed.) Social Networks in Urban Situations. Manchester: Univ. of Manchester Press.

KATZ, E. (1957) "The two step flow of communication: an up-to-date report on an hypothesis." Public Opinion Q. 21 (Spring): 61-78.

——— and P. F. LAZARSFELD (1955) Personal Influence. Glencoe, Ill.: Free Press.

KOSTELANETZ, R. (1974) The End of Intelligent Writing: Literary Politics in America. New York: Sheed & Ward.

LAZARSFELD, P. F. and R. K. MERTON (1954) "Friendship as a social process: a substantive and methodological analysis," pp. 18-66 in Morrae Berger, Theodore Abel, and Charles H. Page (eds.) Freedom and Control in Modern Society. New York: Van Nostrand.

LAZARSFELD, P. F., B. BERELSON, and H. GAUDET (1944) The People's Choice. New York: Columbia Univ. Press.

McPHEE, W. (1963) Formal Theories of Mass Behavior. New York: Free Press.

MERTON, R. K. (1973) The Sociology of Science: Theoretical and Empirical Investigations. Chicago: Univ. of Chicago Press.

MITCHELL, J. C. (1973) "Networks, norms, and institutions," in J. Boissevain and J. Clyde Mitchell (eds.) Network Analysis: Studies in Human Interaction. The Hague: Mouton.

––– (1969) Social Networks in Urban Situations. Manchester, Eng.: Univ. of Manchester Press.

MOKKEN, R. J. and F. N. STOKMAN (1974) "Power and influence as political phenomena." University of Amsterdam, Institute for Political Science. (mimeo)

MOORE, G. (1974) "Preliminary notes on the structure of American leaders." New York: Bureau of Applied Social Research. (mimeo)

MULLINS, N. C. (1972) "The structure of an elite: the advisory structure of the Public Health Service." Sci. Studies 2: 3-29.

––– (1968) "The distribution of social and cultural properties in informal communication networks among biological scientists." Amer. Soc. Rev. 33 (October): 786-797.

NEUMANN, H. et al. (1973) Codebook and Marginals, Leadership in the Federal Republic of Germany. Mannheim: Social Science Research Institute of the Konrad Adenauer Foundation, University of Mannheim.

POOL, I. de S. (1973) "Communications systems," in I. de S. Pool and W. Schramm (eds.) Handbook of Communications. Chicago: Rand-McNally.

PRICE, D. J. (1965) "Networks of scientific papers." Science 149: 510-515.

––– (1963) Big Science, Little Science. New York: Columbia Univ. Press.

ROGERS, E. M. and F. F. SHOEMAKER (1971) Communication of Innovations: A Cross-Cultural Approach. New York: Free Press.

ROISTACHER, R. C. (1974) "A review of mathematical models in sociometry." Soc. Methods & Research 3 (November): 123-170.

SIMMEL, G. (1955) Conflict and the Web of Group Affiliations. New York: Free Press.

––– (1950) Sociology of George Simmel (K. H. Wolff, trans.). New York: Free Press.

SONQUIST, J. and T. KOENIG (1975) "Interlocking directorates in top U.S. corporations: a graph theory approach." Insurgent Sociologist 5 (Spring): 196-229.

TICHY, N. (1976) "Organizations, networks, coalitions and cliques." (unpublished mss.)

––– (1973) "An analysis of clique formation and structure in organizations." Administrative Science Q. 18 (June): 194-208.

VERNON, R. (1963) Metropolis 1985. New York: Doubleday-Anchor.

WRIGHT, C. P. (1975) Mass Communication: A Sociological Perspective. New York: Random House.

ZUCKERMAN, H. and R. MERTON (1971) "Patterns of evaluation in science: institutionalization, structure and functions of the referee system." Minerva 9: 66-101.

*Available evidence marshalled by Useem suggests that natural science, social science, and art have been directly subsidized by the government for quite different reasons. He suggests that the long-term impact of this patronage is to reshape culture production to more nearly fit the needs of government.*

# Government Patronage of
# Science and Art in America

MICHAEL USEEM
*Boston University*

**One of the most rapidly expanding sectors** in American life since World War II has been the government. Local, state, and national government expenditures for goods and services rose from 13% of the gross national product in 1950 to 23% in 1970, reflecting a sixfold absolute increase in government spending. The expansion was not limited to traditional domains, such as defense and welfare. New target areas of government spending include the physical sciences, social sciences, and the arts. Federal outlays for research in the physical sciences rose from $0.6 billion in fiscal 1956 to $2.9 billion in 1963 and $3.8 billion in 1973. Federal support of social science research, which stood at $30 million in 1956, reached $412 million in 1973 (National Science Foundation, 1970: 243; 1974a: 149). Expenditures by the National Endowment for the Arts (1973: 111-112) evidenced a similar trend: initially appropriated $3 million during its first year of operation in 1966, the National Endowment's budget reached $15 million in 1971 and $61 million by 1974.

The institutions engaged in artistic or scientific activity are centrally concerned with the maintenance and extension of cultural systems (Parsons, 1961; Peterson, 1976). The growth of government patronage for these areas suggests that the facilitation and production of culture has become a major state activity in the United States. The objectives underlying this state intervention are not well understood. The central purpose of this paper is to evaluate the relative strengths of several alternative explanations for the government's involvement in the production of culture. A second purpose is to suggest the likely impact of government patronage on the physical sciences, social sciences, and arts in America.

## MODELS OF GOVERNMENT INVESTMENT

Four distinct models for explaining the state's growing interest in the production of culture can be identified. One model emphasizes the value of patronage for the maintenance of the cultural institutions in question. A second model stresses the utility of the investment for capital accumulation. A third model points toward the value of supporting science and art for the administration of government programs. The fourth model identifies the ideological potential of science and art as a primary reason for government patronage.

*Science and art for their own sake.* The first model of government patronage is predicated on the structural-functionalist assumption that the government is a relatively neutral instrument for the articulation and pursuit of collective goals in a society with relatively autonomous subsystems (Parsons, 1969). Pure science and art are vital societal subsystems, and the government moves to protect and develop these areas to ensure the continued production of culture for the benefit of all members of society. Thus, the government intervenes directly as the final patron of public goods that would otherwise be unavailable. Increasingly, the paradigms (Kuhn, 1970: 175) in science and art dictate expenditures that increasingly outstrip the resources of the institutions themselves. Equipment, staff, and data-processing costs of physical science research far exceed the commercial potential of most scientific projects; the cost of conducting systematic and reliable social scientific investigations can no longer be met through product marketing or private foundations; what is more, artistic organizations are increasingly incapable of underwriting all production costs through income and contributions. Under these conditions, government patronage is introduced to ensure the flow of cultural goods to society.

Two important corollaries follow from this formulation, which make it empirically testable. First, the timing of government intervention should primarily be related to economic crises faced by the arts and science themselves, not to crises in the political system, economy, or elsewhere. Second, government intervention should generally take the form of protecting the paradigm of the arts and sciences. Specifically, federal funding should be allocated to the most creative artists and organizations, as defined by the relevant artistic community. Similarly, funding should be preferentially bestowed on scientists whose research is making the greatest contribution to the advance of the scientific discipline, regardless of its relevance for outside problems or crises.

*Science and art for business application.* The second model of government patronage rests on the assumption that "the volume and composition of government expenditures . . . are structurally determined by social and economic conflicts between classes and groups" (O'Connor, 1973: 2). Rather than funding cultural production for its own sake, it is reasoned that the government investment is the product of narrow class or institutional interests. Powerful groups mobilize public funds for their private scientific and artistic purposes. This model presumes that the most powerful interest group in American society is big business. Accordingly, the allocation of government resources to the arts and sciences is seen as the result of large corporate needs for art and science in their business activity. A flourishing cultural climate in a community can facilitate executive recruitment, improve advertising, and attract tourists and conventions. Scientific research is essential for technological advance in industry, particularly among large firms.

The second model, then, holds that the government has invested in science and art in response to, and as a subsidy for, large business firms. Two corollaries follow from this thesis. First, government intervention should accompany sharp increases in corporate consumption of science and art. Second, government intervention should be oriented toward fostering science and art of utility to the large corporation. Federal funds should be disproportionately allocated to individuals, groups, and organizations whose scientific and artistic work has industrial application.

*Science and art for government programs.* A third model rests on the assumption that the government itself has become a major consumer of science and art. It is reasoned, for instance, that "the behavioral sciences are . . . an essential and increasingly relevant instrument of modern government." Utilization of social science research is important because the "decisions of the President, the Congress, and the executive departments and agencies must be based on valid social and economic information" (National Research Council, 1968: 17, 20). Similarly, it can be argued that military weaponry and the space program have been a major stimulus behind government spending on research and development in the physical sciences. The arts are increasingly utilized in government programs as well, according to this model. Applications range from the improvement of federal architecture to preservationist activities and foreign policy.[1]

The national government has entered the field of cultural production, this model suggests, because of the government's own increasing demand for the product that the sciences and arts are uniquely equipped to provide. Corollaries on the timing and orientation of federal intervention follow from the model. First, movement of federal agencies into support for science and art should be associated with increasing government utilization of their products. Second, government support is likely to be slanted toward encouraging science and art of value to government agencies. Federal funding should be preferentially distributed to scientists and artists whose work will be applicable to government programs.

*Science and art for ideological control.* A fourth model for explaining government intervention is built on the premise that ideological control is an important state function. Structural-functionalists and Marxists alike contend that the conduct of government business is facilitated by widespread public confidence in the government (Parsons, 1969; Miliband, 1969). Similarly, both schools hold that shared values and beliefs serve to integrate and preserve the social order. The "value system" or "dominant ideology" mutes social and economic conflicts, reduces aspirations for change, and creates a common definition of societal reality (Parsons, 1961; Lukacs, 1971). As the institution centrally responsible for actively preserving the social order, the national government has a major interest in maintaining both government legitmacy and dominant ideology.

Science and art provide convenient instruments for state efforts to preserve ideological hegemony, according to this model. If government programs are wrapped in the symbols of the physical sciences, preexisting public trust in science and scientists can facilitate public acceptance of otherwise unpopular programs. Similarly, dissemination of social scientific analysis that portrays the American political system as pluralist and based on a value consensus can add legitimacy to government programs, for public policy is seen as serving general needs rather than narrow class interests (Blackburn, 1973).

As representations of social reality, the arts and sciences also perform a socially integrative function (Marcuse, 1966, 1972; Habermas, 1970, 1975). When widely disseminated, they provide a vehicle for communication, a shared definition of the social order, and a common frame of reference for social action. In the breakdown or absence of other integrative symbol systems, the cultural systems of science or art can be used to restore faith in the existing order. Moreover, the arts provide an expressive outlet for otherwise dangerous feelings of frustration and anger arising from the work experience. Antagonism toward the organization of work and other institutions can find a "safe" release in aesthetic expression and consumption (Coser, 1956; Kavolis, 1968).

Science and art are potentially strong instruments for ideological control, and this model asserts that government patronage of both is a product of government efforts to secure new means of ideological control. "This is why," writes Mills (1963: 410), "the cultural apparatus, no matter how internally free, tends in every nation to become a close adjunct of national authority and a leading agency of nationalist propaganda." This model leads to the following corollaries. First, state intervention in the production of science and art should accompany crises in government legitimacy and dominant ideology. Second, government funding should be oriented toward scientists and artists whose work will assist the restoration of the dominant belief system and confidence in the government.

## AVAILABLE EVIDENCE

All four of these models of government intervention in the production of culture are plausible. Each is consistent with some actions taken by the government, but available evidence is sufficient to allow the formulation of more specific, if tentative, assertions about their relative importance.

A fundamental deficiency in most available data on government patronage is that they enumerate only *direct* expenditures. Obviously large, but difficult to calculate, are the innumerable indirect subsidies totaling billions of dollars which facilitate, shape, and inhibit the production of one or another aspect of culture. The operation of tax laws is just one, if the most obvious, case in point. Consider that firms may write off much of the costs of R & D and all of the costs of facilities and equipment through depreciation allowances. Also deducted from taxable income are such regular business expenses as advertising and entertainment expense accounts that underwrite the costs of the major mass media and of popular theater. Contributions to the arts of great advertising value may also be deducted from taxable income. Tax laws also encourage the formation of foundations which, in turn, finance much of the production and mass distribution of culture. Inclusion of indirect support, if known, might change the picture of government patronage sketched here. The best reason for relying on direct government expenditures is that they show changes over time in what the government spends for cultural products which are explicitly requested and legitimated. Nonetheless, the findings reported are tentative, and considerable research will be required to fully evaluate the following hypotheses.

*Physical science for business.* It appears that corporate application is a substantially more important factor in the case of physical science patronage than in the case of support for social science or art. This is suggested by the patterns of federal funding of science during the 1950s. The decade of the 1950s was a period of one of the most massive and most rapid expansions in support of the physical sciences ever undertaken by the national government. Federal expenditures on research and development hovered at a little less than $1 billion annually during the late 1940s, but reached $11 billion by 1963. This coincided with a less robust, but nonetheless substantial, acceleration in corporate financing of R & D. Corporate support of R & D registered a 243% increase between 1953 and 1963, totaling over $5 billion in 1963 (National Science Foundation, 1971a: 3; 1974b: 28-29).

It would appear that it was a period of sharp growth in corporate use of science and technology, and that the federal government moved to subsidize production of the needed scientific research. This is further suggested by the changing shape of government funding during the decade. As the amount of government money increased, a decreasing proportion was allocated to research conducted within the federal bureaucracy, where concern with government utility of the product is likely to be paramount. In 1953, 37% of federal R & D funds were kept within the government, but this proportion dropped to 20% by 1963. Concurrently, an increasing proportion of the government money was distributed to industrial firms, where business applications are likely to be the chief concern. Thus, 52% of the government R & D funds were consumed by corporations in 1953, but this climbed to 65% by 1963. The effect of the transfer is that an increasing proportion of the research conducted in business firms is supported by the government. The proportion of corporate research and development subsidized by the government increased from 39 to 58% during the decade. Similar patterns are evident even when basic research, applied research, and development funds are examined separately (National Science Foundation, 1974b: 20-29). Moreover, these funds are highly concentrated in the largest corporations. In 1967 approximately 11,000 companies had some R & D programs, but the largest 274 firms obtained 90% of the government R & D support distributed to industry (Tybout, 1972; Hill, 1968).

The business application model holds that government intervention in the production of physical science should follow growing large-firm use of physical science, and that government patronage should be skewed toward scientists most likely to yield a research product with business applications. Both patterns are apparent in the available data, but additional evidence is required to adequately rule out alternative explanations for these patterns.

*Social science for government.* If the 1950s were the decade of intense federal intervention in the production of physical science, the 1960s were the decade for social science. The national government's financial commitment to social research stood at $72 million in 1960, but it reached nearly $350 million by 1970 (National Science Foundation, 1971a: 221). Available information indicates that government use of social research has been a more dominant factor in government patronage for social science than for either physical science or art.

The timing of the expansion of social science patronage closely paralleled the growth of federal activism on a variety of social fronts during the 1960s. Government programs were rapidly expanded in domains ranging from poverty to crime, education, and manpower. Concurrently, equally sharp increases were registered in federal funding of research in each of these areas. Federal expenditures on education and manpower programs rose from $1 billion in 1960 to $8 billion in 1970; federal expenditures on education and manpower research grew from $70 million in 1960 to $430 million in 1970. With the exception of a few early years, the amount of R & D outlay remained a relatively constant 6% of the total outlay for manpower and education programs throughout the decade (National Science Foundation, 1971b: 91-93).

The distribution of federal patronage for social science indicates that neither business application nor ideological control have been as important a concern for the government as public policy needs. If business utility were a central concern, a substantial fraction of the federal funds should be allocated to industrial settings where the full potential of social science for business is most likely to be realized. Yet indirect evidence suggests that little federal social research money has been consumed in industrial settings. A 1968 census of scientific and technical personnel found that 24 to 28% of the nation's physicists, chemists, and mathematicians with federal backing were employed in business. By contrast, fewer than 5% of the social scientists with federal funds were located in industry (National Science Foundation, 1969).

More direct evidence on the patterns of federal funding of academic social scientists is consistent with the government application model, but it is inconsistent with the ideological control model. In 1974, I surveyed nearly 1,100 academic social scientists in the disciplines of anthropology, economics, political science, and psychology. A strong predictor of which social scientists receive federal research funds is the policy-relevance of their research, regardless of the purely scientific value of their investigations, their professional reputation, or a variety of other factors. This is the pattern expected by the government application model. On the other hand, the distribution is contrary to that expected by the ideological control model. The political persuasion of the social scientist has no independent effect on the likelihood of receiving government research funds, implying that ideological content has been a comparatively unimportant state concern in social science support (Useem, 1976c).

The evidence is generally more compatible with the government program model than the other explanations of government intervention. The production of social knowledge for social policy is clearly not the sole consideration in the state's backing of social science, but it appears to be more salient than other considerations.

*Art for ideological control.* Direct federal patronage for the arts emerged only after patronage for the sciences was firmly established as national policy. Support for the arts did not begin until the mid-1960s, when the National Endowment for the Arts was created (1965). The belated involvement of the government may appear to be an eleventh-hour effort to rescue the arts from imminent financial ruin, similar to government intervention on behalf of bankrupt corporations. Yet the arts had been a chronically depressed sector for years, and there is no evidence that the 1960s marked a sudden worsening of an already gloomy financial condition (Baumol and Bowen, 1967; Poggi, 1968).

Though the arts were not facing unique circumstances in the mid-1960s, the national government was confronted by a sharp upsurge in political dissidence and decline in legitimacy.[2] The spread of urban disorder and organized protest movements posed a serious challenge to both government policies (e.g., pursuit of the Indochina war) and societal stability. Government agencies resorted to both utilitarian and coercive efforts to restore control. Public relief was used to quell protest among the poor, and coercive techniques—arrest, harassment, and violence—were employed against organized dissident movements (Piven and Cloward, 1971; Balbus, 1973). Ideological control provided a third means of restoring order, and it appears that this consideration may have been a major factor behind initial government intervention on behalf of the arts.

In a speech delivered during the peak of the black inner-city revolts (1968), Douglas Dillon, a former Secretary of the Treasury and chairman of the Business Committee for the Arts, urged that business can no longer afford to focus "solely on science, technology, and finance." Corporations must increase their concern for art, Dillon (1969: 49) argued, because "artistic performances of one sort or another are essential in handling the crisis of our cities." The arts are one of "our most effective tools in the effort to rid our society of its most basic ills—voicelessness, isolation, depersonalization—the complete absence of any purpose or reasons for living."

The crisis of legitimacy, and the potential role of the arts for overcoming it, are recurrent themes in the reports and statements advocating increased government involvement during the mid-1960s. This is evident in a report on the performing arts that played an important role in mobilizing federal commitment to the arts. Authored by a panel convened by the Rockefeller Brothers Fund (1965: 7), the report stressed the arts' utility as a means for proper consumption of leisure time, a vehicle for satisfying the "spiritual hunger" left unmet by the society's political and economic institutions, and a device for structuring meaning in an otherwise "baffling world." Thus, "the use of leisure can be both an individual and community problem if it is not channeled into constructive and satisfying ranges of activity such as the arts afford."

The government's chief arts agency, the National Endowment for the Arts, is prohibited from underwriting artistic work in business firms, suggesting that direct corporate application has not been a major motivating concern in government patronage for the arts. Evidence is unavailable on whether federal funds are more oriented toward those likely to produce art for ideological control or government programs, but it is anticipated that research will demonstrate a preferential funding of the former. While the absence of adequate data makes this case the least compelling of the three, available evidence at least points toward the primacy of the arts' ideological control value as an explanation for state intervention in the arts.

*Cultural production for its own sake.* The fourth working hypothesis states that government patronage to advance the sciences and arts for their own sake is the result of an exchange relationship between the government and these cultural institutions. Support is given the sciences and arts for their own ends in exchange for their cooperation in producing science and art for the government's ends.

Compared with other interest groups, the scientific and artistic communities are ill-equipped to lobby for government programs serving their interests. Their resource base is limited and their political organization is weak. Accordingly, there is likely to be little political pressure on the government to support the sciences and arts for their own sake. However, a special circumstance—the government's dependence on cultural institutions for needed services—permits the sciences and arts to exert substantial influence through other means. It is hypothesized that this influence accounts for the allocation of some government funds to the production of culture as an end in itself.

The national government has relied on the private sector for the conduct of government business in a variety of realms, including the delivery of cultural products (Weidenbaum, 1969; Smith and Hague, 1971). At the same time, science and art have become dependent on the government for financial support. The cost of scientific and artistic work place both beyond the realm of self-financing, making patronage essential. The patronage market in the sciences has become heavily dominated by the federal government. In 1974, federal agencies were responsible for 55% of all research expenditures in the country. One-fourth of the cost of research in industry was underwritten by the federal government, with no other outside source providing any funds. The government's share of research funds consumed in higher education and other nonprofit institutions was 61 and 66%, respectively (National Science Foundation, 1974a: 4-5).

Though the government is responsible for a relatively small share of patronage for the arts, available evidence points toward eventual state dominance of this domain as well. This trend is apparent from a study of the finances of the largest 166 nonprofit performing arts organizations during the 1966-1971 period. Unearned income—support from all outside sources—grew from 41 to 48% of the total income of the organizations. The share of the unearned income contributed by all government units expanded from 8 to 18% over the six seasons, with the federal component growing from 2 to 7%. The average annual growth rate in total operating revenue (constant dollars) of the performing arts organizations was 7% during the 1966-1971 period. By contrast, unearned income was climbing at a 12% annual rate, and federal contributions were increasing 28% annually, the highest growth rate demonstrated by any income source. If current trends continue, by 1981 it is estimated that 66% of total income will be unearned, 40% of the unearned income will be contributed by government sources, and 17% of the unearned income will be given by the federal government alone (Ford Foundation, 1974: 102-110).

Scientists and, increasingly, artists have little choice but to initiate a dialogue with the federal government. The government's reliance on the cooperation of scientists and artists makes it ready for such a dialogue as well. The terms of the resulting exchange of resources will be a function of the relative strength of the two bargaining parties (Emerson, 1962; Blau, 1964). The small scale of the artistic and scientific communities make them no match for the government, but they retain a critical strategic opportunity—they can withhold their services. Moreover, there is an incentive to do so. The priorities of the paradigm are not the same as those of the government, and many scientists and artists will be reluctant to take on work requested by the government that is considered marginal by their colleagues (Robinson, 1971).

One means of encouraging cooperation is to orient some federal funds toward projects of no utility to the government but of great value to the artistic or scientific community. This helps create the impression that government patronage allows some latitude for pursuing paradigm-defined priorities. Moreover, it appears that the government is genuinely committed to the advance of science and art for their own sake. Both impressions encourage and legitimize cooperation with the government.

An informally negotiated exchange of resources and cooperation is established between the government and the arts and sciences, and this implies that two principles should structure the distribution of government money. Some funds should be allocated to those most likely to contribute to the advance of their paradigm, while other funds should be allocated to those most prone to furnish the government with the product it needs. In the case of the social sciences, then, federal support should be oriented toward social researchers likely to advance their own discipline *and* toward investigators whose research will contribute to the formulation and execution of public policy. Both funding patterns are clearly evident in my previously described study of academic social scientists (Useem, 1976a) as well as in the natural sciences (Kuhlmann-Wilsdorf, 1975).

It would appear that science, art, and the government have become mutually dependent on one another's resources, with gains and costs to each. The government secures the type of cultural product it requires, at the price of supporting some irrelevant work to ensure the cooperation of the scientific and artistic communities. The sciences and arts secure the financing they require, including some for priorities of their own choosing, but they also allocate a portion of their resources to government-dictated priorities.

## IMPACT OF GOVERNMENT PATRONAGE

Government patronage oriented toward cultural production for its own sake is likely to have a conservative impact on the paradigms. Dominant styles and approaches are reinforced, and marginal areas are made even more so by the increased resource inequalities. However, government patronage is also a source of change, since much of the money is distributed according to government priorities rather than paradigm priorities. Were this investment minor in magnitude, the sciences and arts would be in a position to resist intrusion of external pressure. But, as we have seen, in the sciences and increasingly in the arts the government's role as patron is preeminent. Full insulation of the paradigms from externally induced change is highly unlikely.[3]

Paradigm change is hypothesized to pass through two stages. In the first stage, the flow of personnel and resources into government-related areas is not sanctioned by the paradigm.

Work on government priorities is viewed as peripheral or inappropriate. Even those undertaking such work tend to see it as a means to some other end, such as their own employment or access to money they might divert to their own purposes. Government cooperation is obtained through material incentives rather than mobilization around shared objectives.

Government criteria are, however, gradually incorporated into the paradigms themselves. Well-endowed fields, even if initially of marginal status, attract participants and develop their own networks and subcultures. In time, associations, training programs, ritual gatherings, shows, workshops, and journals emerge to institutionalize the areas. If through nothing more than their financial strength, these fields soon acquire legitimacy, and their priorities are incorporated into the broader paradigm of the scientific and artistic community. In this second stage, government cooperation is obtained by mobilizing scientists and artists through shared objectives rather than purely instrumental incentives. Government priorities are latently imbedded in the paradigm, and work related to these objectives is no longer viewed as "applied."[4]

In both stages, the most visible impact of government patronage is heightened productivity in government-supported areas and reduced efforts in others. This occurs even though only a minority of the research in the supported areas receives federal funding. Thus, federal money has a leverage effect and an impact well beyond the direct dollar expenditures in assistance. McCartney (1971), for instance, found that sociologists tend to migrate toward well-funded specialties and away from those which are impoverished. My study of four social science disciplines reveals that researchers react to reduced federal funds for their specialties by giving their research a more applied slant, thus making it more attractive to the government, or by changing to substantive concerns receiving federal money (Useem, 1976b). A similar effect can be seen in the allocation policies of employing institutions. Federal outlays have a major influence on the redistribution of resources within universities and research institutes (Lodahl and Gordon, 1973; Salancik and Pfeffer, 1974). The same processes seem to govern changes in the number and subfields of scientists trained and employed in the university system (McGinnis, 1972; Drew, 1975).

The fact of government patronage does not mean that government influence must be all-pervasive. Government interests are not monolithic, foundations and other patrons still have a significant influence, and the interests of culture workers can still shape paradigm development. Yet this brief review of the U.S. experience of the past three decades suggests that the role of government patronage in shaping the production of culture deserves much further investigation.

## NOTES

1. Descriptions of government applications of the arts can be found in U.S. Congress . . . (1965) and Associated Councils of the Arts (1975).

2. National surveys show a steady erosion of public confidence in the government since the early 1960s (Miller, 1974; House and Mason, 1975).

3. Kavolis (1974) concludes that the arts are least capable of maintaining their autonomy when dependent on a small number of large patrons, and it is generally observed that an institution's autonomy is inversely related to the external concentration of essential resources (Evan, 1966; Zald, 1970).

4. This transformation has apparently not been studied in the American arts and sciences since the advent of massive government sponsorship, but studies of science in other settings reveal that such a process is common (Ben-David, 1971; Oberschall, 1972; McVey, 1975).

## REFERENCES

Associated Councils of the Arts (1975) Cultural Directory: Guide to Federal Funds and Services for Cultural Activities. New York: Associated Councils of the Arts.
BALBUS, I. D. (1973) The Dialectics of Legal Repression: Black Rebels Before the American Criminal Courts. New York: Russell Sage.

BAUMOL, W. J. and W. G. BOWEN (1967) Performing Arts—The Economic Dilemma: A Study of Problems Common to Theater, Opera, Music, and Dance. Cambridge: MIT Press.

BEN-DAVID, J. (1971) The Scientist's Role in Society: A Comparative Study. Englewood Cliffs, N.J.: Prentice-Hall.

BLACKBURN, R. [ed.] (1973) Ideology in Social Science: Readings in Critical Social Theory. New York: Random House.

BLAU, P. (1964) Exchange and Power in Social Life. New York: John Wiley.

COSER, L. (1956) The Functions of Social Conflict. New York: Free Press.

DILLON, C. D. (1969) "The corporation, the arts and the ghetto," pp. 48-51 in A. Gingrich (ed.) Business and the Arts: An Answer to Tomorrow. New York: Eriksson.

DREW, D. (1975) Science Development: An Evaluation Study. Washington, D.C.: National Academy of Sciences.

EMERSON, R. M. (1962) "Power-dependence relations." Amer. Soc. Rev. 27 (February): 31-41.

EVAN, W. M. (1966) "The organization-set: toward a theory of interorganizational relations," pp. 173-191 in J. D. Thompson (ed.). Approaches to Organizational Design. Pittsburgh: Univ. of Pittsburgh Press.

Ford Foundation (1974) The Finances of the Performing Arts: A Survey of 166 Professional Nonprofit Resident Theaters, Operas, Symphonies, Ballets, and Modern Dance Companies, Vol. I. New York: Ford Foundation.

HABERMAS, J. (1975) Legitimation Crisis. Boston: Beacon.

——— (1970) Toward a Rational Society. Boston: Beacon.

HILL, K. B. (1968) "Business and science," pp. 236-279 in I. Berg (ed.). The Business of America. New York: Harcourt, Brace & World.

HOUSE, J. S. and W. M. MASON (1975) "Political alienation in America, 1952-1968." Amer. Soc. Rev. 40 (April): 123-147.

KAVOLIS, V. (1974) "Social and economic aspects of art," pp. 101-122 in Encyclopaedia Britannica, Fifteenth ed., Vol. 2. Chicago: Encyclopaedia Britannica.

——— (1968) Artistic Expression—A Sociological Analysis. Ithaca, N.Y.: Cornell Univ. Press.

KUHLMANN-WILSDORF, D. (1975) "Statement," before the Subcommittee on Science, Research and Technology, Committee on Science and Technology, U.S. House of Representatives, July 29.

KUHN, T. S. (1970) The Structure of Scientific Revolutions, Second ed. Chicago: Univ. of Chicago Press.

LODAHL, J. B. and G. GORDON (1973) "Funding sciences in university departments." Educ. Record 54: 74-82.

LUKACS, G. (1971) History and Class Consciousness: Studies in Marxist Dialectics (Rodney Livingstone, trans.). Cambridge: MIT Press.

MARCUSE, H. (1972) "Art as form of reality." New Left Rev. 74 (July-August): 51-58.

——— (1966) One Dimensional Man: Studies in the Ideology of Advanced Industrial Society. Boston: Beacon.

McCARTNEY, J. L. (1971) "The financing of sociological research: trends and consequences," pp. 384-397 in E. A. Tiryakian (ed.) The Phenomenon of Sociology: A Reader in the Sociology of Sociology. New York: Appleton-Century-Crofts.

McGINNIS, R. (1972) Federal Funding and Graduate Program Assistance. Washington, D.C.: Office of Scientific Personnel, National Research Council.

McVEY, S. (1975) "Social control of social research: the development of the social scientist as expert, 1885-1915." Ph.D. dissertation, University of Wisconsin.

MILIBAND, R. (1969) The State in Capitalist Society. New York: Basic Books.

MILLER, A. H. (1974) "Political issues and trust in government." Amer. Pol. Sci. Rev. 68 (September): 951-972.

MILLS, C. W. (1963) "The cultural apparatus," pp. 405-422 in I. L. Horowitz (ed.) Power, Politics and People: The Collected Essays of C. Wright Mills. New York: Oxford Univ. Press.

National Endowment for the Arts (1973) Annual Report, 1973. Washington, D.C.: Government Printing Office.

National Research Council (1968) The Behavioral Sciences and the Federal Government. Washington, D.C.: National Academy of Sciences.

National Science Foundation (1974a) Federal Funds for Research, Development, and Other Scientific Activities, Fiscal Years 1973, 1974, and 1975. Detailed Statistical Tables, Appendices C and D. Washington, D.C.: Government Printing Office.

——— (1974b) National Patterns of R&D Resources: Funds and Manpower in the United States, 1953-1974. Washington, D.C.: Government Printing Office.

——— (1971a) Federal Funds for Research, Development, and Other Scientific Activities, Fiscal Years 1970, 1971, 1972. Washington, D.C.: Government Printing Office.

——— (1971b) An Analysis of Federal R&D Funding by Budget Function. Washington, D.C.: Government Printing Office.

——— (1970) Federal Funds for Research, Development and Other Scientific Activities, Fiscal Years 1969, 1970, and 1971. Washington, D.C.: Government Printing Office.

——— (1969) American Science Manpower, 1968. Washington, D.C.: Government Printing Office.

OBERSCHALL, A. [ed.] (1972) The Establishment of Empirical Sociology: Studies in Continuity, Discontinuity, and Institutionalization. New York: Harper & Row.

O'CONNOR, J. (1973) The Fiscal Crisis of the State. New York: St. Martin's.

PARSONS, T. (1969) Politics and Social Structure. New York: Free Press.

——— (1961) The Social System. New York: Free Press.

PETERSON, R. A. (1976) "The production of culture: a prolegomenon." Amer. Behav. Scientist 19 (July-August): 669-684.

PIVEN, F. F. and R. A. CLOWARD (1971) Regulating the Poor: The Functions of Public Welfare. New York: Pantheon.

POGGI, J. (1968) Theater in America: The Impact of Economic Forces, 1870-1967. Ithaca, N.Y.: Cornell Univ. Press.

ROBINSON, D. Z. (1971) "Government contracting for academic research: accountability in the American experience," pp. 103-117 in B.L.R. Smith and D.

C. Hague (eds.) The Dilemma of Accountability in Modern Government: Independence Versus Control. New York: St. Martin's.

Rockefeller Brothers Fund (1965) The Performing Arts: Problems and Prospects. New York: McGraw-Hill.

SALANCIK, G. R. and J. PFEFFER (1974) "The bases and use of power in organizational decision making: the case of the university." Admin. Sci. Q. 19 (December): 453-473.

SMITH, B.L.R. and D. C. HAGUE [eds.] (1971) The Dilemma of Accountability in Modern Government: Independence Versus Control. New York: St. Martin's.

TYBOUT, R. A. (1972) "Economics of research," pp. 129-160 in S. Z. Nagi and R. G. Corwin (eds.) The Social Contexts of Research. New York: John Wiley.

U.S. Congress, House of Representatives, Committee on Education and Labor, Select Subcommittee on Education (1965) National Arts and Humanities Foundations. Joint Hearings with U.S. Senate Committee on Labor and Public Welfare, Special Subcommittee on Arts and Welfare. Washington, D.C.: Government Printing Office.

USEEM, M. (1976a) "Government mobilization of academic social research." Policy Studies J. 4 (Spring): 274-280.

——— (1976b) "Government influence on the social science paradigm." Soc. Q. 17 (Spring): 146-161.

——— (1976c) "State production of social knowledge: patterns in government financing of academic social research." Amer. Soc. Rev. 41 (August): 613-629.

WEIDENBAUM, M. L. (1969) The Modern Public Sector: New Ways of Doing the Government's Business. New York: Basic Books.

ZALD, M. N. (1970) "Political economy: a framework for comparative analysis," pp. 221-261 in M. N. Zald (ed.) Power in Organizations. Nashville, Tenn.: Vanderbilt Univ. Press.

# THE AUTHORS

**HOWARD S. BECKER** is Professor of Sociology at Northwestern University. He is currently working on problems in the sociology of the arts and in the relation between photography and sociology.

**DIANA CRANE** is Associate Professor of Sociology at the University of Pennsylvania. She is the author of *Invisible Colleges: Diffusion of Knowledge in Scientific Communities; The Sanctity of Social Life: Physicians' Treatment of Critically Ill Patients;* and a forthcoming book on the sociology of culture.

**PAUL DiMAGGIO** is a graduate student in the Department of Sociology at Harvard University. He is co-chairperson of the editorial board of *Harvard Educational Review,* and he has written on the arts and popular culture for such journals as *Social Forces* and *Arts in Society.*

**WARREN O. HAGSTROM** is Professor and former Chairman of the Department of Sociology, University of Wisconsin—Madison. His book, *The Scientific Community,* has recently been reissued by Southern Illinois University Press. His current research includes case studies of scientific revolutions and the organization of research in universities.

**MAX HEIRICH** is Associate Professor of Sociology at the University of Michigan. He is currently studying the impact of nonwestern medicine on paradigm formation in the sciences and on the organization of health care practices.

**PAUL M. HIRSCH** is Visiting Professor of Sociology at Stanford University, on leave from the University of Chicago Graduate School of Business. He is currently engaged in a study of the television medium—its organization, effects, and prospects for change with the advent of new communications technologies.

**CHARLES KADUSHIN,** Professor of Sociology and Education at Teachers College, Columbia University, is currently assigned to the Social Psychology Program of the Psychology Department. He is the author of *The*

*American Intellectual Elite; Why People Go to Psychiatrists,* and a number of articles in the field of networks.

**RICHARD A. PETERSON** is Professor of Sociology at Vanderbilt University. He is currently completing a monograph on the development of the music industry in Nashville, and he is engaged in several other studies in the production-of-culture domain.

**MICHAEL USEEM** is Associate Professor of Sociology at Boston University, where he is completing a study of the structure and impact of government funding of academic social research. Other current research interests include the relationship between social class and higher education in the United States.